"I am thrilled about your new book, *The Spirit Contemporary Life*. Spirit Contemporary brings together both 'power' and 'practices' to engage our constantly changing culture for the cause of Christ. It has been said, 'We don't get to choose the culture we are called to reach for Christ. We get to choose how we are going to engage it.' For example, there was a time when the European and North American church played 'home' games. Yet today, most of the time, the church in these regions plays 'away' games. We can either continue down this path of misconnect or move to Spirit Contemporary and witness firsthand more coming to Christ than ever before."

     —James O. Davis, president of Cutting Edge International and co-founder
        of Billion Soul Network

"I believe *The Spirit Contemporary Life* has the potential to become the 'next Azusa Street,' moving us forward in the winning of our world to Christ through the power of the Holy Spirit. Just as it takes two wings for a bird to fly, it takes two wings for a church or organization to soar. Just as one wing is program, the other wing is power. When it comes to this book, one wing is 'Spirit' and the other is 'Contemporary.' When Spirit and Contemporary are synergized together, phenomenal outcomes will happen in the church. I believe this valuable resource will help the church go to higher levels of impact and influence in the years ahead."

     —Dr. Elmer L. Towns, co-founder of Liberty University

"This timely book shines a light on a truly important concept: the gifts of the Spirit can and should be better adapted to our modern-day culture and powerfully utilized by each and every one of us in our daily lives to minister to those around us. If we dare to adopt this mind-set, we will be more effective, attractive, and culturally relevant. Leon's dramatic personal journey as a former EMT gives testimony to the fact that a 'Spirit Contemporary' life is an exciting, miraculous, and fulfilling way to live."

     —Matt Crouch, chairman of the board of Trinity Broadcasting Family
        of Networks (TBN)

"Leon Fontaine has helped countless leaders in our nation and beyond. His life-giving insights have empowered them to effectively present the timeless message of God's love and power to an ever-changing world. An exciting adventure awaits those who embrace the challenge clearly articulated in this book."

—WAYNE ALCORN, national president of Australian Christian Churches

"I love it when someone can take the complex and make it simple. Pastor Leon Fontaine has put two words—*Spirit* and *Contemporary*—together to create a brand new paradigm of living the daily life we were meant to live."

—SAM CHAND, leadership consultant and author of *Leadership Pain*; president emeritus, Beulah Heights Bible College

"This is the most inspiring book on evangelism, power ministry, and the authenticity of Spirit-led life I have ever read. With numerous personal illustrations, Leon Fontaine takes us into the daily experience of living the life described in the New Testament gospels and letters. Solidly rooted in Scripture, Fontaine helps us explore what it means to live a Spirit Contemporary life personally and corporately as the body of Christ. This is not another book about relevance; this is a book inviting us to live fully in Holy Spirit's presence."

—DOUG BEACHAM, presiding bishop of the International Pentecostal Holiness Church

"Powerful and revolutionary! *The Spirit Contemporary Life* stirs up the best in us and beckons us to live out our highest calling. Here we are challenged to become agents of God's miraculous intervention as He leads us in tune with our current culture without sacrificing our spiritual moorings. Don't pass up this book! It ignites a strategic, life-changing focus!"

—GLENN C. BURRIS Jr., president, The Foursquare Church

"*The Spirit Contemporary Life* reminds us all of our need for the Holy Spirit in our lives on a daily basis. It is a reminder we need daily and this book is the evidence."

—DR. JAMES MERRITT, president emeritus of the Southern Baptist Convention; lead pastor of Cross Pointe Church in Duluth, Georgia; host of the international broadcast *Touching Lives with James Merritt*

THE SPIRIT
CONTEMPORARY
LIFE

LEON FONTAINE

Unleashing the Miraculous
in Your Everyday World

THE SPIRIT CONTEMPORARY LIFE

WATERBROOK

THE SPIRIT CONTEMPORARY LIFE

All Scripture quotations, unless otherwise indicated, are taken from the Holy Bible, New International Version®, NIV®. Copyright © 1973, 1978, 1984, 2011 by Biblica Inc.® Used by permission. All rights reserved worldwide. Scripture quotations marked (AMPC) are taken from the Amplified Bible, Classic Edition. Copyright © 1954, 1958, 1962, 1964, 1965, 1987 by the Lockman Foundation. Used by permission. (www.Lockman.org.) Scripture quotations marked (KJV) are taken from the King James Version. Scripture quotations marked (MSG) are taken from the Message. Copyright © by Eugene H. Peterson 1993, 1994, 1995, 1996, 2000, 2001, 2002. Used by permission of Tyndale House Publishers, Inc. Scripture quotations marked (NKJV) are taken from the New King James Version®. Copyright © 1982 by Thomas Nelson Inc. Used by permission. All rights reserved. Scripture quotations marked (NLT) are taken from the Holy Bible, New Living Translation, copyright © 1996, 2004, 2007 by Tyndale House Foundation. Used by permission of Tyndale House Publishers Inc., Carol Stream, Illinois 60188. All rights reserved.

Italics in Scripture quotations reflect the author's added emphasis.

Details in some anecdotes and stories have been changed to protect the identities of the persons involved.

Trade Paperback ISBN 978-1-60142-870-7
Hardcover ISBN 978-1-60142-869-1
eBook ISBN 978-1-60142-871-4

Cover design by Kelly L. Howard; cover photography by Aaron Foster

Published in the United States by WaterBrook, an imprint of the Crown Publishing Group, a division of Penguin Random House LLC, New York.

WATERBROOK® and its deer colophon are registered trademarks of Penguin Random House LLC.

The Library of Congress has cataloged the hardcover edition as follows:
Names: Fontaine, Leon, author.
Title: The spirit contemporary life : unleashing the miraculous in your everyday world / Leon Fontaine.
Description: First Edition. | Colorado Springs, Colorado : WaterBrook Press, 2016.
Identifiers: LCCN 2016002846 (print) | LCCN 2016005796 (ebook) | ISBN 9781601428691 (hardcover) | ISBN 9781601428714 (electronic)
Subjects: LCSH: Christian life.
Classification: LCC BV4501.3 .F635 2016 (print) | LCC BV4501.3 (ebook) | DDC 248.4—dc23
LC record available at http://lccn.loc.gov/2016002846

Printed in the United States of America
2017—First Trade Paperback Edition

10 9 8 7 6 5 4 3 2 1

SPECIAL SALES
Most WaterBrook books are available at special quantity discounts when purchased in bulk by corporations, organizations, and special-interest groups. Custom imprinting or excerpting can also be done to fit special needs. For information, please e-mail specialmarketscms@penguinrandomhouse.com or call 1-800-603-7051.

I dedicate this book to Sally, my loving wife,
who is my partner in ministry and life.
We both know you are the one who first challenged
our religious thinking! You worked powerfully by my
side, and together we are still walking out this new
adventure called the Spirit Contemporary Life.

Contents

Why Read This Book?

One of my favorite verses in the Bible is John 10:10, which I slightly paraphrase as something like this: "Jesus came so we could get a life."

It's time that we stop living boring, safe little Christian lives and start thinking differently about God, about life, and about ourselves.

It's time to get real. That's why I want you to read this book.

I'm sure you've noticed that the church is not a perfect institution. The church is comprised of human beings, and as long as human beings are part of the mix, there will be problems to solve every day. But the biggest problem the church faces today is the way we as Christians approach the rest of the world on God's behalf.

Our message is fine. In fact, the message is perfect, so we don't need to change it. The message is Jesus, and there is nothing we can do to improve on that message. But sometimes when people share that message, it does not result in others turning to Christ. In most parts of the developed world, the church is actually shrinking.

Why do so many tune out when followers of Christ try to share their faith? Why do our young people fall away from God? Why do many intelligent, well-educated people seem to run from all things Spirit filled? And why don't we see evidence of Holy Spirit's power in the marketplace and on the streets, just as much as we do in a church building?

Since we know that the message about Jesus is perfect and Holy Spirit's power to influence our lives is incredible, the problem has to lie with the messengers. It has to be us.

We are the problem.

There is a simple solution. We can learn to communicate Jesus's message in the context of our normal, everyday lives . . . and we can do it in a way that doesn't send people running.

Can it really be that easy? We tend to assume that no one wants to hear about our relationship with Jesus. We're afraid people will make fun of us. It's risky. Or we overcomplicate things and fall for the lie that it is natural for our methods of sharing our faith to result in criticism or rejection.

So many earnest believers needlessly offend and end up pushing away the very people Jesus has called us to reach. They have the best intentions, thinking that their refusal to bend tradition is how they show God their devotion, but I don't think God sees it that way.

Really, there is a simple and highly effective way to go about it. We can influence others for Jesus while we build great relationships with them. This new culture, this new way of communicating and living out our faith, is something I call the *Spirit Contemporary* life.

To sum it up, the Spirit Contemporary life means living so in tune with Holy Spirit that you are guided and empowered to help others *in natural, authentic, contemporary ways.* It's not just about putting a new face on Christianity; it's about getting back to the basics of what Christianity was always meant to be and then presenting *that reality* to the world.

This book is going to change how you see Jesus and help you discover how you can live in his power every day. You'll read stories of miracles—miracles that didn't take place in church but "out there" where life happens: at accident scenes, on streets, in schools, at workplaces, and in homes. You'll see how God's miraculous power can work through *you* in your everyday life, and it's going to radically change how you live.

You'll witness my own struggle and see how Holy Spirit led me to revolutionize how I approached my faith. Holy Spirit did a complete overhaul on my heart—and it was so simple. If he did it for me, he will do it for you too.

Spirit Contemporary is going to change everything about your life! So . . . are you ready? It's time to embark on an adventure. You can experience more of God's power, peace, and joy as you live each day. You can live in a way that causes people to be attracted to Jesus as they never were before. Not only will this concept change your life, but through it, you can help to completely transform the way the world looks at Christians.

Together, we can change what people think it means to follow Jesus. Let's get started!

Part I

THE PROBLEM

From Altars to Ambulances

The ambulance sped along the highway, two wheels on the shoulder and two in the ditch. Traffic had already backed up for miles on the double-lane highway between the city and the beach. My nineteen-year-old mind darted in a dozen directions, trying to recall my recent training. *Assess the danger. Triage the victims. Maximize survivors.*

I had confidence in myself and my training, but my heart still raced at the thought of what lay ahead. The dispatcher had given us only vague information—a serious accident involving several victims—but news of the wreck was already all over the local radio stations. *This is a bad one,* I thought, praying I would be able to remember my training under the pressure.

As we rolled up on the scene, the driver turned off the siren, and I was struck by how eerily quiet it was—no honking horns or blaring music as you would expect in a long traffic jam. Then, in the distance I heard it, the faint sound of a child crying.

I spotted him as soon as the ambulance stopped: a little boy no more than a year old sitting in the middle of the highway, wearing only a diaper, surrounded by broken glass and debris. A crowd had gathered at the scene, but no one dared go near him, probably because they were afraid of doing more harm than good. People just stood there staring at the toddler in his helpless state, as if they were paralyzed by the magnitude of the damage before them.

The overturned van lying to one side of the highway caught my eye next. None of the passengers had been wearing seat belts, so the impact of their flying bodies had blown out the side of the vehicle. Victims were scattered from one side of the highway to the other like rag dolls tossed by a thoughtless child. Nothing I had experienced before and none of my training could have prepared me for the sights, sounds, and smells that flooded my senses.

Not far from the toddler, a baby lay motionless, his skull noticeably fractured by the impact. After quickly covering the baby, who was beyond help, I assessed the condition of a woman whom I assumed to be the mother. She was alive, but barely. Two men lay beyond her—one dead, the other barely hanging on to life.

At the time I didn't know how profoundly this experience would affect me. Both parents died later that day. The little boy survived, but both mom and dad had been ripped from him in an instant, forever altering his world and, to a certain degree, mine. You see, nothing in my upbringing could have prepared me for the pain and heartache I began to encounter on a daily basis as an emergency responder.

———

Both my mom and my dad were pastors, and as far back as I can remember, they served side by side at the same church. I grew up listening to their teaching, and I have tremendous respect for both of my parents. At our church, miracles were a regular occurrence. I witnessed tumors disappearing, hearing restored, and people walking freely after years of crippling pain. As a little boy, I was always eager to go to church to see what God would do. It was exciting, powerful, and fascinating, and I'm so thankful for the way I was brought up. But now I had come face to face with the heartbreaking reality of emergency rescue.

Some nights, after a particularly traumatic shift, I could not erase the smell of blood or clear the image of a dying child from my mind. My experiences in emergency rescue raised questions that seemed to have no answers. I was confident in

Holy Spirit's miraculous power; I had witnessed it firsthand. Yet now I was faced with a hurting world, with people in desperate need, with blood, and tears, and pain, and death. And the church seemed so . . . irrelevant.

When we prayed for people in church, it was always beautiful and perfectly under control. But at accident and crime scenes, there was no organ music setting the right atmosphere and no pastor to pray. There were just the moans of the sick and screams of the dying and the heartrending sobs of mothers holding dead babies or dads searching for missing children. Day after day this was my reality, and I was completely unprepared for it.

I called out to God at this time in my life, desperately wanting him to show me how to minister to people in the "real world."

It's not that church isn't real and beautiful. I'm a pastor as well as a pastor's kid, and I love church. We pray for the sick in our services every week. But hurting people are everywhere: at your workplace, your school, the grocery store, the gym, an accident scene. Wherever you go, God provides opportunities to demonstrate his love and power to hurting people, even if you don't always know how to respond. Church is not—it can't be—the only place God works.

In my heart I firmly believed God wanted to touch every person's life with the same miraculous power I saw regularly in church, but I was angry and frustrated because the church seemed oblivious to the needs outside its four walls. And I felt powerless to do anything about it. It was great that we all were praying in church, but we did it with worship music in the background, at the altar, accompanied by language and behavior unfamiliar to the outside world. That approach would have

> **I wanted God's power not only in the front of the church but also in the back of my ambulance.**

stuck out like a sore thumb outside the church, not to mention that if I prayed for people that way in the back of an ambulance, I'd have been fired. But I needed to do something! For the first time in my life I was witnessing the painful reality that many people who don't know Jesus live with every day—violence, tragedies, suicides, sexual and domestic abuse—and I had no way to introduce them to the person they so desperately needed to meet. I knew how to be a Christian in church, where everyone spoke the same language and acted the same way, but I had no idea how to bring that faith into my everyday world.

The reality was I wanted God's power not only in the front of the church but also in the back of my ambulance. My heart was breaking. I wanted him to touch people in hospitals, on streets, and in ditches at three o'clock in the morning when I was ankle deep in water and blood trying to save lives. And I wanted to find a way to work in the power of Holy Spirit that wouldn't turn people off. I had seen entirely too much of that in my young life, and I was convinced we could be more like Jesus, who somehow performed incredible miracles *and* attracted people who were far from God. So at that time in my life, when I was balancing the brutal reality of first-response medical aid and faith in a miracle-working God, I asked him to show me how to pray in a way that got results.

I didn't know it then, but what I was longing for was a Spirit Contemporary approach to the Spirit-filled life.

Maybe you can relate. You may have wanted to share your faith, or wanted to reach out to people in need, or wanted to see miracles happen in the lives of others but were afraid you'd be pegged as a weirdo or extremist. Or maybe you do share your faith and invite people to church consistently but can't understand why they don't respond positively more often than they do.

If this sounds familiar, hang on, because you're in for the ride of your life. I invite you to join me in the Spirit Contemporary life.

———

Before we get started . . . one more important point!

You may have noticed I refer to God's Spirit as Holy Spirit and not as *the* Holy Spirit. I do this because Holy Spirit is a person, not some impersonal force. In John 14:16, Jesus referred to Holy Spirit as "another Comforter" (KJV). The word *another* tells us that Holy Spirit functions exactly the same way Jesus did. Jesus didn't leave us with someone less wonderful than he is. He left us with someone exactly like him.

When you think of Holy Spirit, don't think of a blob or a vapor. Think of a person. You would never say *the* Jesus or *the* Leon because Jesus and Leon are names. They represent people, not functions. Referring to Holy Spirit without the definite article before his name is one way to remind yourself that he is a person, and he's someone who wants to have a phenomenal, rock-your-world-completely kind of relationship with you.

2 Ordinary Heroes

It started out as a day like any other. I was helping out in the emergency room at the hospital where I worked, as I did whenever I wasn't out on a call with the ambulance. A few patients had come in, so I was busy starting an IV when a coworker told me that a woman I knew had been admitted with a broken hip. After finishing up the IV as quickly as I could, I made my way over to check on her where she waited for treatment.

As soon as I walked into her room, my stomach knotted and turned. The woman lay on her back on the gurney, her feet hanging slightly over the end. My eyes darted from one foot to the other and then to the woman's face, which was contorted in pain. One of her feet was pointed up toward the ceiling as normal, but it was the other foot that caused my queasy reaction. This foot was facing toward the floor—*completely backward*—and the leg was about six inches shorter than the other. I had seen my share of shockers, but this one sent shivers up my spine.

Knowing I could be called away at any moment, I took a deep breath and walked in. Since I already knew this woman was a believer, I immediately asked if she wanted me to pray for her, to which she nodded appreciatively. "I speak life and healing into this woman's leg in Jesus's name," I prayed quickly, and no sooner did I finish that sentence than I heard a code called out on the PA system. Promising to come back when I could, I rushed off.

About fifteen or twenty minutes passed before I was able to slip away again to check on her. Walking into her room this time, I noticed that something was dramatically different about her. Peeking over the edge of her gurney were two sets of toes facing straight up, in a normal position, with both legs an equal length.

My first thought was, *The doctors must have started to set the bone in place.* But as she began to tell her story, I could tell that wasn't the case at all.

"As soon as you left, a warm feeling came over my leg." She smiled. "First it started to rotate outward and upward like this"—she motioned with her hands—"then, when my toes were facing all the way up, it started to push out like this." She moved her hand down toward her feet.

I have to be honest. The turnaround was so dramatic that I questioned whether I had been seeing things. *Maybe she wasn't as badly injured as I thought?* But later, when I overheard the doctor and head nurse arguing over her x-rays, I knew I hadn't lost it.

"Her leg has to be broken!" the nurse insisted. She had seen the state this woman was in when she arrived.

"There's nothing wrong with her!" the doctor shot back, just as adamantly. "Her x-rays are completely normal. I'm releasing her."

This woman was not only released from the hospital that day, but even more incredibly, she *walked* out!

It was experiences like this one that made me realize something big had changed in my life. Because of some of the heart-wrenching situations I had come across in emergency rescue, I was desperate to work with God in a way that made sense to other people. My heart went out to the hurting people I encountered every day, and I wanted so badly to help. But I didn't know how.

In my search, I came across a message about the Day of Pentecost, and looking back now, I can see how it changed my life. In that message, the speaker shared how in an instant Holy Spirit had completely transformed 120 men and women who were crowded in a room in Jerusalem. I can't tell you why that particular message touched me the way it did, considering I'd heard so many other sermons on Pentecost. I can only say that hearing the message ignited something inside me—a new passion for more of Holy Spirit. My eyes were opened to how incredibly important Holy Spirit is to every believer, and I set out to learn everything I could about him.

Something radically changed in my life as I learned to know Holy Spirit better. I started to pray for people I encountered at the hospital and to see miracles in their lives as a result. I witnessed miraculous healings in homes, on hospitals beds, and on operating tables. For the first time in my life, I was seeing the power of Holy Spirit at work outside the four walls of the church.

This newfound confidence in Holy Spirit changed everything about me—even the way I spoke. The words seemed to pour straight from my spirit whenever I spoke about Jesus. That ability surprised me, but I was even more surprised at the effects of those words. When I prayed for people, things happened that I couldn't explain, and I knew these experiences weren't happening because I was so special. I was just a regular guy working in a hospital, no different from anyone else.

I was discovering that with Holy Spirit, ordinary people can do extraordinary things. It was the start of my Spirit Contemporary journey. And the truth is that if an average guy like me can have some of the experiences I've had, you can too.

The Answer

Before I started my Spirit Contemporary journey, I followed Christ but I'd have to say I lacked power. I had given my life to Jesus as a young boy, but I had not developed an ongoing relationship with Holy Spirit. I didn't know how to let him work through me, especially in the context of my everyday life.

I had witnessed many miracles happen in church services and had seen people give their lives to Christ at the altar on Sundays. I also had become well aware of the great need outside of the church—people who needed healing or who desperately needed to know Jesus. But I didn't know how to join those two worlds.

I knew that being weird, pushy, hyperreligious, or judgmental wouldn't work. If my attempts to pray for people or talk to them about Jesus made them feel uncomfortable, I'd only push them farther away from Christ. The honest truth is that many methods of evangelism come across this way. To nonbelievers we may seem manipulative, condescending, and self-serving when we talk about Jesus, and that was the last thing I wanted—as I know it's the last thing you want too. We never intend to come across like we're trying to close a deal or get another notch in our evangelical belts.

I was determined to find an effective way to help people. My heart broke for those hurting people around me. You may not be an ambulance driver, but you come face to face with hurting people all the time. And there are hundreds more around you in desperate need that you haven't yet met. Not far from you lives a woman who spends every day cowering in fear of her abusive partner. She lives in isolation, convinced she isn't worthy of love and that no one cares. Down the street a husband and wife, brokenhearted over their daughter's addiction to heroin, watch helplessly as the dreams they had for their little girl die a little more each day.

These people are surrounded by believers just like you and me who really do care. Caring is not the issue. The problem is we often feel helpless to make a difference. You may want to reach out but don't know where to start. Maybe you've only seen outreach done in ways that make these hurting people feel worse, or ways so radical and strange that they drive people away. You want to help, but how?

The good news is there is an answer, and it's simple. The answer lies with allowing Holy Spirit to work through you in a contemporary way in the context of your normal, everyday life. And it can happen so naturally!

NORMALLY AND NATURALLY

When I first began this journey of working with Holy Spirit in my everyday life, I started to see frequent miracles in response to prayer everywhere I went. I didn't need to change my personality to become someone I wasn't, and it wasn't something I had to work up through some emotional experience—it all happened naturally.

One example that comes to mind happened as I met with an alarm-system salesman at a coffee shop. He was a great guy and very good at his job; so good, in fact, that he sold me one of his systems at the end of our meeting! As he explained the features and benefits, I kept getting the sense that he wasn't well. Little nudges and impressions hinted that he was dealing with a health issue, and they kept getting stronger. By the time he had finished his presentation, I was confident I knew what was wrong.

"Do you have a problem with your neck?" I asked.

He admitted he did and was a bit surprised I had noticed. Seeing he was open, I kept going. "Do you have a problem with your lower back and hips too?"

He seemed taken aback. "Is it obvious by how I'm sitting?"

I assured him he didn't look strange, which made him all the more eager to know how I could tell. All the while this was going on, I kept getting more specific information from Holy Spirit, which brought me to my next question: "Do you have a growth in your neck—right there?" I asked, pointing to a specific spot on his neck.

Nothing was visibly out of the ordinary on his neck, so he was shocked. "How did you know that?" he whispered. His curiosity was piqued.

I explained that I was a Christian and that God loves and wants to help people. "Sometimes he helps us know things," I said, "and I had a feeling about you so I thought I would take a risk and say it."

Hearing that God loved him enough to show me a few things about him seemed to resonate with this man, and he began to open up to me. He told me he used to have a relationship with Christ but had stopped pursuing it. As we sat in that coffee shop, he rededicated his life to Jesus, and I was able to pray for him for healing.

Instantly he was healed of the pain in his neck, lower back, and hips, and he was amazed and so grateful to God. But as he felt around his neck, he could tell that the growth was still there. Seeing a bit of disappointment on his face, I assured him, "Don't worry if it didn't disappear right away. Just keep thanking God and it'll go."

Three months later he called to tell me the growth was completely gone.

The thing to realize as you pray for people is that when Holy Spirit works, it's not really about you. It's not about your ability or lack thereof. The more you realize that, the more free you will feel to step into others' lives to help, and the more you will communicate and act in a way that effectively reaches others.

We often assume that we need to be willing to create a scene to work with Holy Spirit. But when I was talking to this man, I didn't need to stand up in front of the entire coffee shop and embarrass him by drawing attention to the situation. I simply needed to submit myself to Holy Spirit so he could work through me.

Just as Holy Spirit began to work in my life, he wants to work in your life as well. You can get to know him a little more every day, as I did, and be led by him in incredibly powerful ways. And as you learn to hear him more clearly, you'll discover how rewarding it is to see him work through you to transform others. Of course, in order to begin this journey, you will need to get to know Holy Spirit personally.

HOLY SPIRIT IN YOU

It must have been amazing to follow Jesus when he walked our planet. He performed incredible miracles that stunned the crowds who flocked to hear him speak. He was as comfortable conversing with common people and society's outcasts as with the wealthy and powerful. He had access to a power far beyond anyone's natural capability, which enabled him to do the impossible—calm storms, walk on water, and even raise the dead. Jesus was undeniably led by Holy Spirit.

The disciples had seen Jesus cast out a demon from a man so deranged that chains couldn't hold him. When I think of this story, I try to imagine it in living color, so allow me a little creative license. I imagine that this man ran full force toward Jesus in his crazed state, stopping dead right in front of Jesus. All the disciples were probably lined up single file behind Jesus for protection, and yet Jesus stood there with complete confidence, and he set the man free. This is the kind of power and confidence the disciples witnessed in Jesus.

With Jesus as their leader, you would think that the twelve disciples would have become an unstoppable team. After all, they had witnessed Jesus's example, had seen the unbelievable miracles he performed, and had been trained for more than three years by the perfect teacher. But when you examine how the disciples behaved while Jesus was with them, you see a very different picture. They were hopeless!

Of the twelve men Jesus personally trained, only one had even a vague idea who Jesus really was (see Luke 9:18–20). Another was stealing money from Jesus and eventually betrayed him. All but one abandoned him when he hung on the cross. Peter, the one you would expect to have the most intestinal fortitude, denied that he even knew Jesus after his arrest. Not only did the disciples let Jesus down but so did the crowds of people who had witnessed and received miracles, heard his teaching, and eaten the free food he miraculously multiplied.

Where were the five thousand who witnessed the miracle of the five loaves and two fish? Where were the people who were healed or who had their sight or hearing restored? Where were the leprous dads who had no hope of ever touching their kids again or of being with their wives before Jesus healed them? They all abandoned him. (See Matthew 14:14–21; Matthew 4:24; John 9:1–7; Mark 7:32–35; Luke 17:11–19.)

True, there was a lot at stake. The disciples' lives were in danger just because they knew Jesus. Even so, those who had gained the most from Jesus seemed to abandon him the quickest. How could that be?

Actually, it's not surprising at all. Although the disciples had given their lives to Jesus, they didn't have access to the power of Holy Spirit at that point. They couldn't have, because Jesus hadn't sent Holy Spirit yet. So although the disciples had good intentions, they had absolutely no access to the power of God that comes from knowing Holy Spirit. They were all operating on their own strength.

That all changed on the day of Pentecost.

Before his crucifixion, Jesus explained to the disciples that Holy Spirit would soon come (see John 14:26), and he reminded them again after rising from the dead. He said, "Do not leave Jerusalem, but wait for the gift my Father promised, which you have heard me speak about. For John baptized with water, but in a few days you will be baptized with the Holy Spirit" (Acts 1:4–5). Jesus told them to stay put because he knew they were hopeless without Holy Spirit.

Ten days after Jesus ascended into heaven, Holy Spirit arrived. He made his entrance in a room full of believers gathered in the upper room of a house, waiting. And when he came, they experienced life-transforming power for the first time, and the change was dramatic. Right afterward, Peter, who previously had been afraid even to be identified as a follower of Jesus, stood in public and preached a bold message that inspired more than three thousand people to follow Jesus (see Acts 2:41). Soon after that, Peter and John preached messages that led about five thousand others to become followers of Christ (see 4:4).

What made so great a difference in the disciples? They already knew Jesus. They had already determined to follow him. Why were they so bold and so effective now?

The big difference was that they now had Holy Spirit empowering them, which changed everything. They didn't abandon their faith when confronted by threats or problems. Their conviction was so strong that eventually many of them gave their lives for their faith because they refused to renounce Jesus or stop talking about him. Not only the disciples but also men, women, and kids were tortured and fed to lions, and yet we do not find a record in the Bible of any of them recanting their devotion to Jesus. The cowering, fearful followers of Christ were gone, and in their place were powerhouses who began to act like Jesus—*Spirit Contemporary!*

This same power can be yours!

I want it to be absolutely clear that you cannot hope to live the Spirit Contemporary life without Holy Spirit. You need Holy Spirit just as much as the disciples and followers of Jesus did. Power and confidence radiated from the apostles' lives after Holy Spirit filled them, and it will do so from your life as well when you allow him to lead you continually. You can access his supernatural power every day, in your ordinary, daily life, and it will enable you to do far more than you could ever do on your own—more than you have ever dreamed possible!

> **The supernatural and the miraculous can become a part of *your* everyday experience!**

I'm not saying you're going to have to become a missionary, pastor, or healing evangelist. That's not what it means to allow Holy Spirit to lead you. If he leads you to one of those callings, that's great. But *everyone* can live the Spirit Contemporary life, not just pastors and evangelists!

Jesus said signs and wonders would *follow* those who believe (see Mark 16:17–19). That means these signs go wherever you go—work, school, home, the mall, the gym, the grocery store. They don't occur only at church or on mission trips. The supernatural and the miraculous can become a part of *your* everyday experience as you learn to live the Spirit Contemporary life.

Interested?

3 · It's **NOT** the Message

Several years ago, a woman asked me to visit her father in the hospital. He was in a comatose state and had only days to live, so the family had been called together and were keeping vigil at his bedside around the clock. I asked for a few more details, and after explaining the situation a little further, she quietly admitted, "You should probably also know that none of my family wants you to come."

Since I had never met her family, I was a bit confused at first but she soon clarified: "I think I've been a little too, you know . . . 'out there' in talking about my faith." This woman had the best intentions when it came to attempts to reach her family, but something about her approach had rubbed them the wrong way. Judging by her own statement, she already knew what it was.

Unfortunately, this problem is all too common. We can often get so excited about our relationship with Jesus that we forget to see the other person's perspective. Desperate for friends and family members to spend eternity in heaven, we can push, prod, or manipulate them in an attempt to introduce them to Christ, which unfortunately turns them off entirely.

Sometimes we seem to speak a language others can't understand. Using words like "righteousness," "grace," and "salvation" or talking about the "blood of the lamb" are fine when talking with fellow believers who understand those terms, but those words sound like a foreign language to people who didn't grow up in church. Not only is speaking this way confusing but it can even make people feel disrespected.

I wasn't sure how badly this woman's family had been offended, so while I did agree to pay a visit, I made it clear that if her family didn't want me there, I would respect their wishes and leave.

Later that day I knocked on the door of the hospital room and was met by the woman's brother. A fairly large group of family members were gathered in the room, and as soon as they saw me standing at the door their faces changed. They knew who I was, and I could tell they weren't happy I was there.

Showing great respect for their pain, I offered to leave immediately if that was what they wanted. I also explained that their sister had invited me to come, then asked, "For her sake, would you mind if I just say a thirty-second blessing?" My sincerity must have come through in those words because their faces softened and they invited me in.

As I approached the father, who was lying comatose on the bed, I recognized signs that death was near. I had seen this many times before in my work in emergency rescue: blue lips and a rattling sound as he breathed. A red star on his chart indicated Do Not Resuscitate.

I laid my hand on him and prayed, "Bless this man, Father. I ask you to touch him. Help this family through this terrible time. Give them strength and peace. Fill this room with your peace and presence." My prayer took less than thirty seconds, as I promised, after which I turned to thank the family and let them know our church would continue to pray for them. But before I had a chance to speak, the father, who wasn't expected to regain consciousness before his passing, sat straight up in bed.

In a loud voice, he said, "This is a man of God. I want you to listen to him."

Jaws dropped and the room became suddenly silent. Needless to say, the family was shocked. Actually, so was I!

Through this amazing miracle, their hearts were opened to hear about Jesus. I spent almost an hour with that family, sharing how much Jesus loves and cares for each of them.

Holy Spirit wanted to touch this man and his family. Although the woman who had called me had the best intentions, her past behavior had almost closed the door to what Holy Spirit wanted to do. Yet when I worked in cooperation with Holy Spirit to communicate his compassion, love, and acceptance in a respectful way, the door was reopened.

The truth is that anyone could have done what I did; I simply took the family's feelings into account. Being Spirit Contemporary isn't hard. All you really need is to do two things: respect people and follow Holy Spirit's lead.

IT'S THE MESSENGERS!

As I travel to different countries of the world, I often encounter people attempting to share their faith. You've probably seen them too: people standing on street corners screaming, "The end is coming," or preaching some other version of a "turn or burn" message. Or maybe as you were walking through a public area you noticed someone handing out little pamphlets or tracts. You can just tell by people's reactions to these Christians that their methods aren't going to be effective.

Despite their best efforts, many of these well-meaning evangelists actually do more harm than good. They're stuck in a rut of confrontational techniques that simply don't work. These may be great people who have all the right intentions, but when it comes to sharing their faith, their us-versus-them approach pushes away more people than it attracts.

It isn't that people are opposed to their message. When it's shared the right way, you can't find a more beautiful message than the news about Christ. We as followers of Christ just have to change the way we're sharing it. In other words, *it's not the message; it's the messengers.* But the good news is we can change our approach and people will want to know Jesus as a result!

That's the beauty of the Spirit Contemporary life. When you stay tuned in to what Holy Spirit is saying to you, he will open doors into the lives of people—right here, right now. Instead of being condescending or condemning, sharing the good news with others becomes as natural as stepping into a room. When you live the Spirit Contemporary life, you open the door to what Holy Spirit can do through you, and here's a hint: it's far more than you've ever imagined (see Ephesians 3:20).

The first step is always to begin with respect. This is really the key to being contemporary. It's not about following some sort of formula. It's about listening to Holy Spirit in the moment.

Being contemporary is not a matter of adopting a certain style of dress or type of music. In fact, being contemporary might look completely different from one situation to the next, depending on the context. What's contemporary in Afghanistan is not contemporary in Canada. What was considered contemporary twenty years ago is not contemporary today. Being contemporary requires you to put yourself in other people's shoes, then act in a way that makes them feel accepted, understood, and comfortable.

The apostle Paul understood this well. When he was with Jews, he respected Jewish traditions, but around Gentiles he adopted other customs. That doesn't mean he was fickle or hypocritical, and he certainly didn't compromise his beliefs. He just adjusted his style to make others comfortable and was culturally relevant by being "all things to all people" (1 Corinthians 9:22).

Being contemporary involves looking at the world through someone else's eyes, and Holy Spirit helps you do this effectively. When you take this approach, he can work through you, which is both incredibly exciting and very humbling. You can trust him and let him work through you to do what he's trying to do.

OPEN WIDE

One day, I answered the door at my house and came face to face with a man who looked like a biker. He had long hair and dark sunglasses, and his forearms were covered with tattoos. Judging from his uniform, I could tell he was a courier making a delivery, but the angry look on his face made me think he would rather punch me than talk to me. He handed me a package, and as I signed for the delivery I got a strong sense there was something deeper going on in his life. One word rose to my mind: *suicide.*

I've come to recognize occasions when Holy Spirit is trying to tell me something, but I always proceed with caution. The last thing I want to do is announce that I've heard something from God only to find out I'm way off base. So when I think I'm hearing from Holy Spirit, I communicate it in a way that lets people know I could be wrong.

With this tough-looking courier, however, I had no idea how to casually bring up the fact that I thought he might be about to commit suicide. But because I've learned to trust Holy Spirit when he shows me things, I took a chance and simply said, "Don't do it, man."

"What?" he said, looking confused.

"Just don't do it," I replied.

He let out a few words I'll choose not to repeat and asked me again what I was talking about, this time seeming more agitated.

I calmly responded, "Don't kill yourself."

His expression instantly changed from anger to shock, and he stood motionless. I wasn't sure what would happen next. I didn't think I had missed the mark, but I wondered if he would just storm off, call me crazy, or even become violent. Instead, he glanced around quickly to make sure no one was watching, then whispered, "I was going to do it after my shift today. How . . . how did you know?"

I said, "I'm a Christian. Maybe not the type you've encountered before, but I follow Jesus. Sometimes, when I meet people God is trying to speak to, he'll show me things. Sometimes I miss it, but it looks like today I heard right."

He was visibly shaken, and it took him a minute to process what I was saying. When he was finally able to respond, he said, "You really think God cares enough about me to tell you that?"

I could see his heart was wide open, so I invited him to have lunch with me. We had a great conversation about how much Jesus loves him just as he is. By the time we finished our meal, he had given his life to Christ.

It happened quite naturally. We heard no angels singing the "Hallelujah Chorus." I didn't get spiritual goose bumps, and I didn't bind the spirit of suicide or command demons to flee in Jesus's name. I didn't have to recite ten Bible verses or explain how dinosaurs fit with biblical history or engage in a deep theological discussion. Holy Spirit opened a door into this man's heart, and all I did was follow his lead. I shared a very simple message—Jesus loves you—and anyone who knows Jesus could have done that.

Holy Spirit is able to lead you in a very normal and natural way without drawing undue attention to yourself. Nowhere in the Bible does it say you have to behave strangely to be led by Holy Spirit. In fact the apostle Paul's writing on this subject seems to indicate that the early Christians who did act in weird ways when claiming to follow Holy Spirit were really copying one another, not Christ (see 1 Corinthians 1:10–13). In the same way, many believers today take their cues from other believers rather than from Jesus. We copy the words and actions of others when we should be using Jesus as our model.

The Spirit Contemporary life is about showing your passion for Jesus in a culturally appropriate manner. When you do that, it will appear quite natural to others, and it will attract them to Jesus.

———

Being contemporary opens the door to what Holy Spirit wants to do through you. When I was in the hospital, I didn't rebuke the family for lacking faith or say, "As a man of God I have the right to pray wherever I want." Instead, I spoke in a natural, respectful way so others could relate to what I was saying. I weighed the circumstances, the environment, and the feelings of those involved before venturing in. Nothing could be more contemporary than acting appropriately for the context at hand, and the results were amazing.

When the courier driver knocked on my door, I didn't switch to Elizabethan English and declare, "Thus saith the Lord," although I'm not knocking how that phrase has been used in the past. But in this day and age, we need to speak and act in a way that matches our surroundings so Holy Spirit can be free to release his power in every situation.

Holy Spirit is not asking us to sacrifice all our influence with people to be led and empowered by him. He wants to use that influence, not destroy it. He's asking us to be Spirit Contemporary—to be connected to him in a way that allows us to access his power, but also in a way that enables us to be contemporary so we can gain influence in the world to spread the news about him.

When people think of Christians, they don't think of people who walk in in-

credible power and confidence every day. Words like *excellent* and *wise* don't come
to mind. People don't turn to the Bible for practical answers to the problems they
face. And when they think of "church,"
they don't picture a place that's vibrant,
fun, and full of life—the best place to
grow and build great relationships.

> **Christianity is meant to be the most powerful, attractive force on the planet.**

Instead, when they think of Chris-
tianity, they just see religion with its judgment; condemnation; and empty, old, boring traditions. Either that or they picture the Hollywood show–type behavior they've
seen on Christian TV, complete with "miracles" that they're sure have been staged.

Christianity is meant to be the most powerful, attractive force on the planet. If
we ever hope to redefine it in the eyes of the average person, we need to change our
approach drastically. After all, if people don't like what they see when they look at us,
why would they want anything to do with Jesus? They need to want what we have
so they can discover that Jesus holds the answers they're looking for.

I hope you can learn from these examples and grasp something that took me
many years to understand, a truth that changed my life and my church forever. Holy
Spirit is contemporary! He will lead you to be involved with others in ways that are
completely natural to you. And when you step through those open doors, lives will
be transformed.

4 Stop Marketing Yourself

One warm summer day as my family arrived home from a day at the beach, my daughters, Eden and Danielle, raced each other toward the small steel gate in our front yard. True to their competitive nature, both girls wanted to be first through the gate.

Eden, being a little older and faster, reached the gate a second before Danielle. Danielle, who was about two years old at the time, lunged for the gate but mistakenly reached for the wrong side. I heard a shriek that sent shivers down my spine, and I raced to my daughter's side. One of her tiny fingers had been caught in the metal hinge. The skin and tissue on her ring finger had been scraped back to expose the joint, which was crushed flatter than a dime. As her other tiny fingers curled, this finger remained completely straight because of the damaged joint.

A friend who had spent the day with us at the beach quickly joined me and bent down to assess the damage. When he saw the mangled flesh and exposed bone, his face went as white as a ghost, and he looked like he was going to pass out. Instead, he rushed back to his car and began madly emptying lawn chairs and beach toys from the vehicle to prepare for a quick trip to the emergency room.

I held Danielle in my arms while she sobbed uncontrollably. Ever so gently, I took her little hand in mine and prayed a simple prayer: "Be whole in Jesus's name." Immediately, her screams stopped, and as she often loved to do at that age, she began to play with my mustache.

I looked down at her finger, and although I could still see bare bone where the skin had been scraped back, the joint was no longer crushed. It had been restored to its normal shape and size, and the finger curled naturally alongside the others.

I motioned to my friend, still madly emptying his car, and indicated that I was taking Danielle inside the house. We went straight into the bathroom, where I sat her on my knee and began to pray and worship quietly as I ran water over her finger. She was in no pain and happily played in the water. It was a surreal moment, and I quietly thanked God for the healing I could tell was taking place.

After a few minutes, my friend followed us in to see what was taking so long. Danielle had been so content and I was worshiping quietly, so I hadn't looked at her finger again. Immediately, the look on his face told me something big had happened. Tears were welling up in his eyes and rolling down his cheeks.

When I turned to look at Danielle's finger, I saw that beautiful new skin had completely covered the knuckle. The new, white skin was surrounded by skin that was tan from the summer sun. Only about four minutes had passed, and she was completely healed.

This was an incredible miracle, yet it happened normally and naturally. No organ music played in the background. I didn't loudly command the joint to re-form or the skin to reappear. Any onlookers would have seen nothing more than a father comforting his child.

This miracle came about during a period of time when I had started questioning: *Could miracles happen in such a natural way that they could occur anywhere, with anyone? Were my preconceived notions about how Holy Spirit worked really accurate?*

Now, fueled by the excitement of witnessing Danielle's healing, I began to read the miracle stories in the Bible with fresh eyes. I also started to pray with people at my job. As a result, I began to see that not only does Holy Spirit work miracles outside the four walls of the church—but he does it every day.

You may be thinking, *That's great that those things happened to you, but you're a pastor. I'm just a regular person.* You need to know that things like this happen to people just like you every single day! Every Sunday at Springs Church we read off a list of miracles our church members sent in that week. Would you like to know how many of those people I visited to pray for personally? None! While we do have pastors on staff who visit people in hospitals and in their homes, the vast majority of the praise reports we share tell the story of everyday people reaching out to the people in their world or praying for their own needs and getting miraculous results.

Some of these stories are absolutely incredible—unbelievable financial miracles, relationships restored, healings from terminal illnesses, divine protection from would-be fatal accidents, and recoveries from mental illnesses. Others tell the tale of a loving God who looks after even the smallest details of our lives when we believe and walk in the authority we've been given in Christ. Honestly, some of those "smaller" miracles touch people to a greater degree. We serve a God who isn't too busy or too indifferent to get involved in the smallest details—intervening to help someone get a job that has better hours, healing a wart on a child's foot, or causing a headache to disappear when a little boy prays for his mom.

The truth is that anyone can live the Spirit Contemporary life—including you!

No Audience Required

One day as I walked through the hospital in my uniform, I ran into a family I knew from our church. Their grandmother had been hospitalized and was not doing well, so they asked if I would pray with her.

I had already taken some heat from my boss for praying with people while I was working, so I agreed with one condition: I told them I couldn't pray for her in her room, where I might be caught. If they wanted me to pray for her, they would need to get her to the hospital chapel. They seemed hesitant but they agreed to try, and I emphasized they could tell no one about this, not even the nurses.

I made my way over to the chapel while they headed back to the room to get Grandma. After waiting more than a few minutes, I started to wonder if they were ever coming. Then, off in the distance, I heard a strange, repetitive tinging sound. It was coming from the hallway, and it seemed to be getting louder.

Peeking my head out of the chapel door, I instantly located the source of the sound. As it turned out, Grandma had suffered a massive stroke and half of her body was paralyzed. To get her to the chapel, the family had transferred her to a wheelchair, but she was unable to sit up straight and her arm hung limply at her side. The sound I heard was her thumb hitting the spokes of the wheelchair as they pushed her toward the chapel!

I took one look at her and thought, *Oh boy. What did I just do?* Realizing I had no choice but to go forward, I went over the plan with the family one more time. I would pray, then leave quietly. They should wait a couple minutes before returning Grandma to her room. It seemed like a good plan—but things didn't quite go that way.

I laid my hands on Grandma and began a very simple prayer. But before I had said more than two or three words, she let out an ear-piercing scream. Panicking, I did the only thing I could think to do—I bolted out the door! Once outside the chapel, I whisked my way nonchalantly down the hallway and didn't look back.

It seemed no one was onto me, but I took the added precaution of moving to another floor and working for a couple of hours before daring to check on Grandma. When I finally did sneak back up to her room, I was absolutely shocked to find her walking around the room, packing her bags. She had been released from the hospital!

As far as the doctors could tell, nothing was wrong with her, which they found extremely confusing. They had told the family she had suffered a massive stroke, which would leave her partially paralyzed for life. Now she looked perfectly normal.

As she smiled and chatted with me, I discovered why she had screamed so loudly. The moment I laid hands on her, the numb side of her body began to tingle like a foot that's waking up after falling asleep. Since one whole side of her body had been affected, the sensation was overwhelming. After about a minute it subsided though, and by the time her family had pushed her back to her room, she was able to get up and walk to her bed.

This is just another experience that proves we can pray for people in normal, natural ways and still see amazing results. There's no need to put on a big Hollywood show to usher Holy Spirit's power into the situation. We don't need to draw attention to ourselves, because it's not about us. Even when we're praying in secret, hoping *not* to be noticed, Holy Spirit can do his work. The interaction is between God and the person who needs him. No audience required.

> There's no need to put on a big Hollywood show to usher Holy Spirit's power into the situation.

In the book of Acts, we see that the apostles worked with Holy Spirit to heal people in a natural way. Although incredible miracles happened at their hands, they never put on a show. They were ordinary people who behaved in ordinary ways, yet they did incredible things that brought people to Christ.

Somewhere along the way, however, some Christians developed the idea that miraculous healings always created a kind of spectacular event. Today, many people add a touch of Hollywood drama to their prayers, which only draws attention to them and away from Jesus. This is the opposite of what we should be doing! In fact, when you look at the way the apostles handled things, they were very concerned with ensuring the *opposite* result. They wanted to direct all the credit back to Jesus.

When Paul and Barnabas preached at Lystra, they were horrified when the crowd directed attention to them instead of Jesus. Seeing that they had healed a man, the locals started to worship Paul and Barnabas as gods. The two men ran through the crowd, tearing their clothing and yelling, "What do you think you're doing! We're not gods! We are men just like you" (Acts 14:15, MSG).

These apostles didn't announce themselves as healers or claim to be special in any way. First of all, they wanted Jesus to get the credit he deserved. Second, they realized that if the people thought Paul and Barnabas were gods or superheroes of some kind, they would assume the healing miracle could not be replicated. If only certain superholy people can pray for healing, then the rest of us have to depend on them, not on Jesus. Yet Jesus clearly stated miraculous signs would accompany all who believe in him: "They will place their hands on sick people, and they will get well" (Mark 16:18).

When we "spectacularize" Holy Spirit's work, we make it seem as though God only works through certain special people who are uniquely gifted. By doing this, we draw attention away from Jesus and place it on ourselves. Instead, we should have the

attitude of John the Baptist, who said, "He needs to become greater; I need to become less" (John 3:30, my paraphrase).

The truth is that you don't have to try to look spiritual to get incredible results.
Not only that but you will also come across as more real and authentic, and Holy
Spirit will have greater freedom to work through you. You don't have to try to convince people that God speaks to you. You don't even need to announce it. When he
does work through you to touch people, they'll be asking you for answers, and your
source will become obvious to everyone who needs to know.

UNFORCED

Many years ago I was invited to speak at an event in northern Canada, and since I
had arrived early in the day, the pastor who invited me took me around town to visit
a few residents. When we knocked on the door of one tiny, dilapidated house, we
were met by an elderly First Nations (aboriginal) woman who spoke a bit of broken
English. As we stood in the doorway and chatted, I caught a glimpse of her husband
sitting in a wheelchair near the red-hot potbelly stove in the middle of their living
room.

The woman introduced us to her husband, but by the look of disgust on his face,
it was obvious he wasn't impressed that the pastor and I were there. He didn't speak
English, so she explained he had been in the wheelchair for years. She also mentioned he didn't believe in Jesus. We invited them both to join us for the meeting that
evening, but before we left, I asked if I could pray with the man. He grunted a response, which she translated: "Many men have prayed for my leg."

I'm not one to push myself on people, so I was about to turn to leave when I
sensed that the problem wasn't in his leg but instead in his brain. I communicated
this to his wife, and when she translated it, the man became angry. Through a bit of
discussion, I realized he thought I was saying that the problem was psychosomatic or
"all in his head."

I explained quickly that I believed he had a physical problem but the origin of
that problem was in his brain—maybe due to a stroke or an aneurysm. This was a

new thought to him, and hope seemed to flicker in his eyes at this possibility. Again I asked if I could pray for him, and this time he agreed.

Standing beside the man, I prayed a simple prayer for healing to take place in his brain. As soon as his wife had finished translating my prayer, I said, "Just to see, why don't you try moving your feet?"

There was no mood lighting in the room and no special effects. I didn't command him to get up out of his wheelchair and walk. I just asked him to try to move, as if we were having some fun and trying it out. When I looked down, his feet were moving slightly.

His wife shot up from her crouched position beside him and shifted back and forth from one foot to the other excitedly. "He's never been able to do that!"

"Well, that's kind of interesting," I responded. "Can you lift your legs?" He pulled one leg out of the stirrup on the wheelchair, and it landed on the ground with a *thud*. As his wife screamed something about this being a miracle, I said, "Do you want to stand up?"

His wife lifted under one arm and I lifted under the other, and he rose to his feet. He stood there swaying for a minute, then growled something in his language about wanting to walk. I didn't need to say "Walk in the name of Jesus" or anything like that. I simply watched in amazement as he took a couple of steps, then barked something else at her as he shook free of her arm. He wanted her to let go of him. Again his wife reached out to steady him, but again, he shook her off angrily and refused to let her help him.

I was thinking, *We can't let go of him! He's going to fall right on this red-hot potbelly stove he's walking around!* But he wouldn't take no for an answer. He shook us both off and made his way haltingly around that hot stove.

That night he walked to the meeting on his own strength. He looked like the Pied Piper because of the line of awestruck people that followed him.

God wants to use each one of us to touch others, but we don't have to force it to happen. Isn't it so freeing to know that you don't have to raise your voice or scream at the devil? Holy Spirit can work through you normally and naturally!

And there's no need to promise healing. I can't think of a single instance where

I promised healing or any other type of miracle. It is not necessary to make outlandish claims like "You are not going to die" or to shout "Get up out of that wheelchair" in order to see miracles happen. And you don't need to tell people to stomp on their glasses, throw away their hearing aids, or go off their medication to receive healing. When our kids were sick, Sally and I used to joke that we would pray for healing and then anoint them with cough syrup, pain medication, or whatever they needed to manage their symptoms while the power of God was healing them.

In most cases where I have been involved in a healing, I've spoken to people in a normal, conversational way. We laugh and smile, and I teach them a bit about what the Bible says about healing and God's kindness. The interactions are relaxed and as natural as breathing.

When I have visited someone in the hospital and the nurses asked me to leave, I've always respected hospital rules and instructions from staff members. Acting in this contemporary way has never prevented God from touching the lives of the people. In fact, anything but this respectful approach draws attention to me and takes the focus away from Jesus.

The more we try to work up some unusual phenomenon, the less effective we become. Just let Holy Spirit do what he wants to do in any situation. You never have to force Holy Spirit to work.

THE RIGHT FOCUS

The apostle Paul gave us a surefire way to make sure we don't get off track with ministering to others. He said there is one thing even better than being used by Holy Spirit—*love* (1 Corinthians 13:13). It's a good thing to earnestly desire to be empowered by Holy Spirit to do miraculous things, but loving others is even more important. If our motivation is love, we won't get caught up in making ourselves look important. Instead, everything we do through Holy Spirit will be done in a way that best serves others.

Jesus is in love with people, and he wants to work through us. He wants to heal moms who have cancer, bring peace and hope to suicidal teenagers, and provide solid direction to business owners on the brink of bankruptcy. When people feel lost and alone, Jesus wants to bring comfort and direction. And he wants to do all of this in a normal, natural way . . . a Spirit Contemporary way.

The problem, however, is that the Spirit Contemporary life involves change. We've become so accustomed to thinking that cooperating with Holy Spirit means putting on a big show or behaving in some spectacularly different way that it now seems normal to us, or we avoid Holy Spirit altogether because we don't want to be labeled as weird. And it's misbeliefs like these that are the biggest deterrent to becoming Spirit Contemporary.

Don't be afraid of this new way of thinking about Holy Spirit and how he works with us. You can learn to embrace change and, as a result, enjoy the freedom of walking through the doors Holy Spirit opens in front of you. You *can* enter this new, exciting way of living! But first you need to understand why you are resisting the changes you need to make to become Spirit Contemporary. We'll talk about that next.

Part 2

FREE TO CHANGE

5 Feeling Strange Is Good

What we're doing isn't working.

Many churches in North America close their doors each year because people are tired of religion. They're not interested in being judged and shamed into submission, and the next generation is falling away from the church because it doesn't speak their language. We are not relating to young people where they are or showing them how to solve real problems in their lives.

The Spirit Contemporary life is the solution. Believers who live in a Spirit Contemporary way are able to meet people where they are and respond to their needs, guided by Holy Spirit, in a powerful yet relatable way. This approach is incredibly effective for bringing people to Christ, because it taps into our innate sense of purpose and joins us in a partnership with Holy Spirit. It is an exciting way to live!

So, if being Spirit Contemporary is so great, why isn't every follower of Christ living this way? The reason is simple: living the Spirit Contemporary life requires change, and people avoid change because it makes them uncomfortable. It challenges their belief systems and makes them feel incompetent, which isn't a great feeling.

To enter the Spirit Contemporary life, *you need to confront your fear of change.*

CHANGE FEELS STRANGE

I encountered this fear when leading Springs Church through monumental changes in our church services. When we first started to make changes, such as allowing people to raise their hands and pray in their seats to give their lives to Christ rather than coming forward to pray at the altar, many church members became very upset. They would approach me with tears in their eyes and tell me they just didn't feel right about the change. They felt that Holy Spirit was telling them we had compromised our faith. They were so tied to familiar ways of doing things, even though we had found better, more efficient methods. They had wrapped their faith in Jesus so tightly around those familiar methods that in their minds, throwing out the methods meant tossing out their faith as well!

At first this bothered me a lot. We were doing our best to reach people who didn't know Jesus, and the last thing I wanted to do was compromise my faith. Yet I knew I had to take direction from the Bible rather than from my experiences or the opinions of others. I couldn't find a single example in the Bible of people coming to an altar to begin a relationship with Jesus, and this gave me peace. My heart had been steeped in religious tradition too, but as Holy Spirit helped me understand God's Word, I was able to discern between negotiable methods and nonnegotiable truth.

The reality is, things that make you uncomfortable aren't necessarily wrong. Change always feels strange, even when it places you smack-dab in the middle of God's will.

Actually, refusing to change when change is necessary is one of the most destructive things you can do. Spouses who refuse to change when confronted with behaviors that are destroying their marriages essentially choose to end their marriages. Patients who won't change after doctors warn them about their destructive lifestyles choose to have major health crises. Churches that refuse to change despite all the warning signs that their approaches are failing to reach nonbelievers for Christ effectively refuse to reach others. Change is always difficult but it's also necessary. We have to change to live this Spirit Contemporary life and to fulfill our purpose in this world.

Rather than waiting for painful consequences to direct change, you can go after the truth, accept your current reality, and seek a Spirit-guided solution. After all, it's better to seek change before change is forced on you. Sometimes that means looking for better ways of doing things even when the current systems *appear* to be working.

Years ago I read a book by Robert J. Kriegel and Louis Patler titled *If It Ain't Broke . . . Break It.* In direct opposition to the old saying "If it ain't broke, don't fix it," the authors proposed that some things, even things that seem to be working, need to be changed for the sake of improvement. After all, just because a system is working does not mean there isn't a better, more productive way of doing things.

FIVE REASONS YOU MAY RESIST CHANGE

The ability to embrace change and lead people into change is absolutely vital for becoming Spirit Contemporary. To reach the point of embracing change, you will have to confront the reasons you are resisting it. Here are a few.

Pride

People only change when they can admit there is something they don't know—a truth they haven't yet discovered, a problem they're not aware of, or a better way of doing things. Realistically, there is always room for improvement, no matter how good you are. So don't be opposed to finding new and better ways to live your life.

Fear

Change always involves an element of risk, so it always brings fear. A certain degree of nervousness is normal when facing change, but fear should not prevent you from moving forward. Deal with the fear of change by asking "What if?" What would likely happen if you refuse to embrace change? What could result if you do? What are the possible consequences and benefits of each action?

Rebellion

If you have a rebellious attitude, you'll oppose change not because you disagree but because you don't like to be led. Rebellion is really a form of pride. You won't embrace change until you change that attitude. Don't buck change just because it was someone else's idea.

Laziness

You might resist change because you're comfortable. If you are content to keep things as they are, you won't make the effort to learn a new way of doing them. Remember that it's not all about you. People will spend an eternity without Jesus if you (and I) don't do the work that change requires. Change for them.

Ignorance

You may resist change because you don't see the need for it. You may assume the next generation—your own children—will love Jesus just because you do. They won't. Every generation needs to come to faith in its own right. To lead them there, we have to stay one step ahead. If you still aren't aware of the need for change, keep reading. This book will both open your eyes to the need for change and present you with a better, more effective way to reach the people in your world for Jesus.

———

Change is vital to the Spirit Contemporary life because being contemporary requires us to be ever changing. This is an area of real struggle for the church because we tend to find something that works and then camp out there. That's never effective in the long term because what works today won't in the near future. The world will never stop changing.

> **God is leading us on a journey to know him better.**

God is leading us on a journey to know him better. He will cause us to grow and become more effective. He will lead us to change. Churches need to change. People need to change. Families need to change to keep up with their growing kids. Change may be uncomfortable at times, but if we don't change, we risk losing it all.

Frankly, change has been a struggle for me too. I always believed Holy Spirit's leading would produce a sense of peace, and that certainly is true. But there will be times of discomfort as you walk in step with Holy Spirit, and that doesn't mean you're on the wrong track. I felt absolute terror during many of the changes in our church and often cried out, *God, help me!* Yet I always came back to peace and confidence knowing I was following Holy Spirit's lead in keeping with God's Word.

Overcome your resistance to change by exposing yourself to the truth. Seeing the truth gives you the right perspective and empowers you to change where necessary. To discover truth, you need to take an accurate, thorough look at your thoughts, beliefs, and actions. That means an honest examination of your personal belief system. And that's your next challenge in embracing the Spirit Contemporary life.

6 Controlling Misbeliefs

You already have everything you need within you to become Spirit Contemporary.

Jesus was Spirit Contemporary, and if you have made a decision to follow him, you have the "mind of Christ" (1 Corinthians 2:16, NKJV). Actually, when you made him your Lord, you became an entirely "new creation" (2 Corinthians 5:17, NKJV). As a result, everything you want to become, you already are because of Christ.

I'm not saying that you become perfect the moment you give your life to Christ. You still have habits and beliefs to change. But before you work on any of those external behaviors, you need to start seeing yourself as the Spirit Contemporary person you already are inside. You need to change what you believe. In other words, the reason you may be continuing to resist this change to the Spirit Contemporary life is your personal belief system.

Everyone has a personal belief system. Some are based on truth; others are based on half truths, mistaken ideas, or outright lies. If left unchallenged, these misbeliefs will hinder you from hearing from Holy Spirit, make you less effective at sharing your faith, and prevent you from seeing Holy Spirit's miraculous work.

To become Spirit Contemporary, you need to examine your belief system and challenge any mistaken, limiting beliefs you've picked up from others or developed through your own experiences. But first, let's take a look at the tremendous power of your beliefs to change your life—for better or worse.

DEADLY BELIEFS

One day while I was starting an IV for a woman who was scheduled for surgery, she started to panic. Growing more and more distressed by the minute, she kept repeating, "I'm going to die. I just know I'm going to die."

Glancing at her chart, I reassured her that her surgery was routine and she had nothing to worry about. It didn't help. She kept getting more anxious and agitated, and before long, alarms on her monitoring equipment started blaring. Judging by the readings, I could see that her heart had begun to beat dangerously out of rhythm.

Doctors and nurses flooded into the room, and after a few tense moments, she was stabilized. When her surgeon heard of the sudden change in her condition, he rushed over. He seemed baffled. She had been completely stable just moments earlier, and nothing in her history provided an explanation for this event.

When the surgeon found out that I had been with this woman when her condition took a turn for the worse, he turned his attention toward me. "What happened?" he asked, seeming annoyed. When I described how she kept saying she was going to die, he responded, "Take her off my slate. I'm not touching her."

This woman believed she would die on the operating table, and her surgeon recognized the power of that belief. This belief in her heart affected her physical state to the degree that it almost killed her.

Every belief you hold brings an accompanying result in your life. If you believe Jesus is your Savior and he died for you, you will be saved. As a result, heaven will be your eternal home, and you gain the ability to create an amazing life here on earth. On the other hand, if you believe you are stupid, lazy, or a failure, that belief will create negative consequences in your life. You will begin to live out who you think you are. If you believe you can't make relationships work, you won't create a happy marriage. Your beliefs largely determine the outcomes in your life.

BASED ON TRUTH

I'm not talking about fleeting thoughts here. Some thoughts enter your mind—doubts, misgivings, possibilities, ideas—but they don't stick around. Other beliefs go deeper, residing in your heart even at a subconscious level.

These heart beliefs have been developing throughout your life. Some result from your upbringing. The influence of parents, teachers, church, siblings, and friends have shaped what you believe. Other beliefs were formed from emotionally charged events in your life. Tragedies and failures as well as victories and joyful occasions all produce strong emotions that cause us to interpret our world or to label ourselves in a certain way. Although these beliefs exist on a subconscious level, they produce deep feelings that are hard to shake. Examining these deep feelings can provide clues to your personal belief system.

For example, you can be in a room filled with people and still feel alone. You could be in Disneyland, the "happiest place on earth," yet feel unhappy. You could be famous and enjoy the admiration of millions yet feel like a loser who will never fit in. These deep feelings are telltale signs of the deeper beliefs of your heart.

The consequences of these deep beliefs can be profound. They determine how we see ourselves, as Proverbs 23:7 indicates: "For as [a person] thinks in his heart, so *is* he" (NKJV). They also determine the actions we take and, therefore, our future. That makes it crucial to guard our hearts against false beliefs, as Proverbs 4:23 instructs us: "Above all else, guard your heart, for everything you do flows from it."

Sadly, religion creates many of our misbeliefs.

Because our beliefs are so powerful, our enemy, the devil, loves to get us to believe things that are wrong. We all have these misbeliefs, so we need to work consciously to line our beliefs up with God's Word.

Sadly, religion creates many of our misbeliefs. For example, mistaken religious ideas have caused many to view God as judgmental and angry rather than gracious and loving. When people view God negatively, they become negative, judgmental, and angry themselves. As a result, they live far below their potential. This misbelief has hindered countless people from coming to know Jesus. They want great lives, not miserable ones, so when they see how miserable some Christians are, they avoid Jesus. As a result, they miss out on the life of adventure, joy, peace, and health that Jesus provides. It is vital we get our personal beliefs right. If we don't, we'll never be effective at sharing Jesus and living the amazing life he has for each of us.

One of the faulty beliefs I had to face early on was a mistaken idea about how people give their lives to Jesus. I had always thought that when people genuinely surrendered their lives to Christ, they would be crying, weeping messes. If they prayed the salvation prayer with tears and strong emotion, I knew God had touched them deeply. If not, I thought that they hadn't really made firm decisions for Christ.

Then I started to notice something. Some of the people who sat in our services week after week before calmly raising a hand to indicate they'd made a decision for Christ became very faithful members of our church. Meanwhile, some of the people who expressed their love for Jesus with strong emotions were the quickest to leave when difficulties came. It became clear to me that outward emotional reactions are not the best indicator of a person's heart. Correcting this misbelief freed me to lead people to Christ wherever they happened to be. We could pray in a restaurant, on the street, or anywhere else because there was no need to work up an emotional reaction in order to have a genuine experience with God.

What are your heart beliefs? How do you identify them? Which of them are based on God's Word, and which have resulted from your experiences, your upbringing, or the traditions of your particular church? As you keep moving your heart beliefs toward being based on truth, you free yourself to live the Spirit Contemporary life.

Lemon Trees Don't Give You Cherries

While walking through the halls at our church after a New Year's service, I passed a guy I knew and asked him a typical New Year's question: "What do you think this year's going to be like?"

He called back, "Oh, it is going to be the best year ever!"

A couple months later, we crossed paths again, and I asked how things were going. He said, "It is just another stinking year, just like I thought."

He was speaking the right things, believing for good things for his future, so why didn't they take shape in his life? It's because his first statement was from his head, but the second was from the heart.

He was trying to produce cherries from a lemon tree.

What do I mean? Well, as I mentioned before, paying attention to your deep, abiding feelings will give clues to your deepest beliefs. A second indicator of your personal belief system is the fruit—or result—of your beliefs in your life. Jesus said, "A tree is recognized by its fruit" (Matthew 12:33).

In other words, you can tell a lot about what you believe by looking at what those beliefs produce in your life.

A lemon tree produces lemons. No matter how much you want cherries, you will never find them on a lemon tree. In the same way, *a misbelief will not produce good results in your life because it can't.* So if you can't seem to get the results you want in a particular area of your life, you likely hold a misbelief in that area.

Our deepest beliefs are usually formed without conscious actions on our part, as we've seen. However, these beliefs, right or wrong, always result in outward behavior. Jesus said, "A good man brings good things out of the good stored up in his heart, and an evil man brings evil things out of the evil stored up in his heart. For the mouth speaks what the heart is full of" (Luke 6:45). Whatever you believe deep down in your heart, you will experience in your life. Your heart is your control center—whatever is going on in your heart eventually becomes visible in your life.

Much of what happens in life results from these heart beliefs, yet few people take the time to understand what they believe to ensure it's right. More often we simply blame our circumstances when things go wrong. But your circumstances don't control your life; your beliefs do.

What does your behavior indicate about your deepest beliefs? What clues to your personal belief system can you find in the fruit—the results—in your life? Make no mistake, the two are related. Your deepest beliefs are powerfully shaping your life. Are those beliefs in line with God's truth?

———

The life you have right now is a snapshot of your heart. If you hold a misbelief in your heart, no positive affirmation or self-talk will change your life. That misbelief will produce negative results because it comes from your heart.

It's time to deal with your belief system by going after the truth in God's Word. If you are struggling to change, you're not alone. We all have a few misbeliefs to tend to. Allow Holy Spirit to work within you. Spend time meditating on his Word. Find a life-giving church and become part of that growing community. Study to find out the beautiful plans God has for you and how much he loves you. God's plans for you are filled with his favor and goodness. He loves you, forgives you, and wants the best for you. Begin to believe the truth, and the truth will set you free in any area of your life (see John 8:32).

7   Spiritual Birth Control

On the journey to becoming Spirit Contemporary, you're going to encounter quite a few new thoughts, and some of them will make you uncomfortable. That's because confronting misbelief involves change, and change is always difficult. But if you want to go to places you've never been, you'll have to think things you've never thought.

One small example of this occurred in my life the first time I preached wearing jeans. I had been raised to believe that wearing my best clothes to church was a sign of respect for God, but times had changed. People were dressing much more casually both at work and at church, and I knew it was more important to make people feel comfortable in church than abide by an outdated, man-made rule. Besides, God was much more concerned with what was going on inside of me than what I chose to wear on the outside. Knowing that "people look at the outward appearance, but the LORD looks at the heart" (1 Samuel 16:7), I put on my sharpest-looking jeans and suit jacket and headed to church on a Sunday morning.

Here's the funny thing: even though I knew in my heart this was a good decision and perfectly in keeping with God's Word, I still felt uncomfortable for a while. When I look back on it now, preaching in jeans was a very small thing. But I had to deal with what I believed before my behavior—and, eventually, my feelings—would come into line.

Many people hold beliefs that limit them, beliefs that don't line up with God's

> **If you want to go to places you've never been, you'll have to think things you've never thought.**

Word. These misbeliefs function like a form of birth control, preventing the birth of all the wonderful new things God wants them to access in their lives. They would begin to beautifully and naturally produce the awesome, exciting kind of life that God has for them if they would only deal with their misbeliefs. These limiting misbeliefs fall into one of four categories. So if you're trying to identify and correct the misbeliefs carried in your heart, this is the place to begin.

THINK BIGGER

One way Holy Spirit regularly works on our beliefs is by challenging us to think bigger, because misbeliefs are often characterized by small-minded thinking. In fact, when you read the Bible, you can see how God always seems to expand our thinking before he uses us.

When God called Moses to deliver the Israelites from slavery in Egypt, Moses complained, "I've never been good with words. . . . I stutter and stammer. . . . Oh, Master, please! Send somebody else!" (Exodus 4:10, 13, MSG). In response, God told Moses he would put the necessary words in his mouth (see verse 12). God equipped Moses with the ability to perform signs and wonders that caused many to believe. In addition, God promised that upon leaving Egypt, the Israelites would plunder the Egyptians of their wealth! Moses was thinking small; God showed him a much bigger vision.

What about Joshua? He must have had the tendency to think small because God kept telling him, "Be strong. Take courage" (Deuteronomy 31:23, MSG). God had to change the way Joshua thought because his thinking was limiting his life—and his ability to lead.

And think of Gideon—now he was a man with low self-esteem. When the angel called him a "mighty man of valour" (Judges 6:12, NKJV), Gideon said, "Who, me? I'm the lowest man in my family and my family is the lowest in the land" (verse 15, my paraphrase). Yet God saw Gideon as a great man, and he wanted Gideon to see himself that way too.

Esther had a new thought that changed her life. She won a beauty contest and became the favorite wife of the Persian king Xerxes. Then one day someone gave her a new thought. Maybe she didn't inherit incredible looks just so she could live comfortably as queen. Maybe she was created for a much greater purpose—to save God's people.

Abraham had to think differently too. God promised Abraham a son when he was one hundred years old and his wife Sarah was ninety (see Genesis 17:16). Sarah laughed out loud at the thought of it, but when she and Abraham started to expand their thinking, they saw that prophecy fulfilled. When you believe something new, you begin to do new things, and your actions move you toward a new future.

Jesus caused his disciples to think differently about nearly everything. He did a complete overhaul on what they believed about God, the results of sin, forgiveness, leadership, and the kingdom of heaven. In just three and a half years, their thinking was torn apart and then built up far bigger than before. These uneducated men became leaders of a movement that has transformed the world.

The world is full of small thinkers. My Australian friends call it the Tall Poppy Syndrome, meaning that small thinkers have a tendency to criticize highly successful people—anyone whose head sticks up above the crowd—and cut them down to size. If you succeed in business, unsuccessful people accuse you of cheating. If your church experiences growth, small-minded people think you have compromised the truth.

When you have a big dream, these small thinkers will tell you to be realistic. Or they may say, "Oh, I tried that. It'll never work." Their thinking limits them to "the way it's always been." The reality is that God wants each of us to live great big lives filled with joy, purpose, and significance. After all, Jesus said he came so you and I could "get a life" (John 10:10, my paraphrase). Isn't that exciting? We aren't destined to live boring, mediocre lives! In fact, if a believer feels stuck in a monotonous day-to-day, it's only because he or she is afraid to think differently and take a chance on something new.

Where do you find yourself thinking small? When you hear of others' successes, are you able to celebrate with them or do you feel envious? What do you sense Holy Spirit leading you to do but feel afraid to try? These are indications of small thinking. Challenge that misbelief by thinking bigger.

SHOOT THOSE HOLY COWS

When I'm challenging a man-made religious belief, I like to refer to it as a holy cow. It's a tongue-in-cheek way of describing a religious belief people hold that has become so ingrained in their thinking that they no longer question it. These are prime examples of misbeliefs that become limiting and harmful, and the best thing to do with a holy cow is shoot it.

For example, many people have preconceived notions about what it means to be led by Holy Spirit. Based on their experiences or the behavior they've seen in others, they think Holy Spirit always produces some sort of emotional behavior or "show" in the people he speaks to. So that behavior becomes a holy cow—something that can't be questioned or even examined. While some people truly have had emotional experiences prompted by Holy Spirit, we can't assume that he *always* leads people that way or that the unusual behavior by itself is evidence of Holy Spirit's work. As a result of this misbelief, many people are turned off by the very idea of Holy Spirit's leading. That holy cow has done enough damage in the church.

Putting on an elaborate show, screaming, ranting, and acting out in bizarre ways has caused a great deal of misbelief. It's no wonder many level-headed people stay far away from churches that teach about Holy Spirit. Let's shoot this holy cow right now: Holy Spirit does not lead people to behave strangely. That's a misbelief.

Another holy cow has to do with the traditions of the church. I'm not talking about the beautiful traditions of the church that have biblical basis. I mean the empty traditions that many confuse with essentials of the Christian faith. Because they fear compromising on core beliefs, some Christians claim their way of doing things—their programs, their style of music, or their way of worshiping—is *the* way. Their traditions become holy cows, practices that are not to be questioned even though they can find no biblical basis for them.

Some would say that altering these traditions is a form of compromise, but in reality, being contemporary has nothing to do with compromising truth. Being contemporary is simply adapting yourself and your communication style to the culture that surrounds you. It's changing the packaging but not the contents of the package. It is adapting the way you share Jesus while remaining fully committed to the essentials.

There will always be some who dilute the gospel to attract a crowd, but not everyone who wants to be contemporary does that. You can tell those who do because they leave out critical parts of the message, such as the uniqueness of Christ, that he's the only way, the fact that we are saved by grace through faith, or the reality of heaven and hell. Those who compromise on nonnegotiables think they're being relevant, but they become irrelevant because they have nothing to offer. Their message becomes increasingly weak and void of the power to transform people's lives.

Truth is relevant. Being Spirit Contemporary does not mean stripping the gospel of its simple truth. To do so would be to strip it of its power to transform lives. Jesus died for our sins on a cross. He was raised to life and sits at the right hand of God. He is coming again to bring eternal life to all who believe. It is not compromising to communicate these timeless truths in contemporary ways.

Are you willing to let go of the holy cow of "the way we've always done it" and let Holy Spirit guide you into truth? You can be Spirit Contemporary and change the wrapper (how you share the message) while leaving the gift (Jesus) intact.

EMBRACE GRACE

Small-mindedness and holy cows are two areas of misbelief you'll need to confront before you can embrace the Spirit Contemporary life. Some other misbeliefs don't seem at first glance to have anything to do with being Spirit Contemporary. In fact, they seem quite biblical. But these beliefs also prevent people from experiencing the amazing life they could have in Christ. We can summarize these beliefs with a single word: *judgmentalism*. Judgmentalism is a sure sign of misbelief. To overcome it, you need to learn to embrace grace.

What is grace? Unfortunately it's a word that is often misused. For instance, if you are about to eat, you might ask, "Who wants to say grace?" But that's just thanking God for your food. That's not grace in the literal sense. In the Bible, "grace" means God's power at work in you—his ability in you, his blessing, his miracles, his peace, his joy, his full provision for your life. And his grace comes to you undeserved.

Now, this is important because in most religions and in religious Christianity, people are continually trying to be good enough to get God to help them out. When many pray, they try to barter with God based on their own goodness: "Dear God, I've been to church five times this year. I put twenty bucks in the plate. Come on! Do something here, God!" It's as if we're trying to convince God that we're good enough for him to do something for us. That's not how grace operates.

When you study grace in the Bible, you can see that it's something God gives as a free gift to every believer—unearned. This is so important because legalistic religion would have you believe that you have to earn God's blessing. It's not true. Jesus died in your place, and when you give your life to him, his grace is yours!

I have a favorite analogy I like to share to try to help people understand what Jesus did for us. The story is about a dad and his rebellious son who left home and was living his life far from God.

One day the dad woke in the middle of the night to someone banging on his front door. When he opened the door, his estranged son fell through it. He was covered in blood.

Between labored breaths the son managed to get across that he had killed a man. "I didn't mean to, Dad," he said, tears streaming down his cheeks. "And now the police are chasing me!"

Immediately, the dad told his son to take off his blood-stained clothes and change into a clean set. "I'll look after these," he told his son. "Now run!"

The dad also instructed his son to go into hiding and not to contact him until he said it was safe to do so. What the son didn't know was that when the police followed his trail to his dad's door, they found his dad *wearing* the blood-stained clothes. Naturally, he was accused of committing the crime, to which he pleaded guilty.

His dad ended up paying the price for his son's crime—and he paid with his life. The son didn't find out until it was too late to do anything about it. Although his beloved son had done something unspeakable, the dad was willing to die in his place so the son could be free.

This story is a Spirit Contemporary way of sharing what Jesus did for us. Jesus took our sin. He put on the sinful clothes of our "crimes." He took the punishment for it all—murder, adultery, stealing, lying, pride, arrogance, gossip—and paid in full. People need to know that Jesus died in their place, for every imaginable sin possible, and when he did, he made it possible

> There's nothing anyone can do that's going to shock Jesus. He's absolutely in love with every person on this planet.

for God's grace . . . his power . . . his love to flow into their lives, if they accept him.

No matter what they've done, it's been paid for. There's nothing anyone can do that's going to shock Jesus. He's absolutely in love with every person on this planet. So if Jesus is that gracious and we are to be like him, there's no room for judgmental attitudes in our lives.

Judgmentalism turns people away from God in droves. It turns people away from church too. Meanwhile, the Jesus whom we serve . . . the Jesus whom we've invited into our lives . . . the Jesus who has become our best friend . . . the Jesus who is our Savior and our Lord . . . is so caring, so understanding, and so beautiful. People need to know the Jesus we know!

Because of judgmentalism, many people wrongly believe God is angry with us. They picture God scowling, banging a gavel, and saying, "Guilty! Guilty! Guilty!" No wonder they want to avoid him. They don't think God wants a relationship with them, and they can't imagine why they would want one with him. They can't picture God blessing them or their work because they think he's angry and disappointed with them.

An offshoot of this thinking is the belief that they pay dearly for every wrong they've ever done because God is always on the lookout for ways to punish wrong-doing. If they break one of his commandments, he will find a way to pay them back. So whenever something bad happens to them, such as getting into an accident, they conclude God orchestrated it as a punishment for something they did.

That thinking springs from the misbelief that God is angry and vengeful. Not only is that thinking biblically inaccurate but it also destroys people's relationship with God. It's true that there are natural consequences to many of our actions. But those consequences are not orchestrated by God; they are simply what happens when certain principles are broken. For example, if you jump off a roof and break your leg, it's because you ignored the law of gravity. You can't blame God or assume that your broken leg is some sort of punishment for jumping off the roof. It's just a natural consequence.

As a teenager, I struggled with the misbelief that God is an angry God, which made me work hard to try to get rid of all the sin in my life. Tears would stream down my cheeks as I sang songs that pleaded with God to search my heart and cleanse me from all my wicked ways (see Psalm 139:23–24). It all seemed very spiritual, but I was mistaking my sad feelings for Holy Spirit's work. I became convinced he was continually condemning me for my sins, and I believed I had to work much harder to make God love me. Later I discovered that condemnation is never from God. God convicts the world of sin only to show them how badly they need Jesus, who is the doorway to forgiveness and healing. God is never out to get us.

This idea that I had to earn my way into God's good graces produced another bad result in my life: it caused me to be judgmental toward others. I would see people laughing and having fun and think, *They ought to be praying or telling others about Jesus.* Without realizing it, I was becoming more like a Pharisee and less like Jesus. Sadly, some Christians love the idea that God is angry because it gives them a reason to feel self-righteous. They seem to think it's their job to bring his anger everywhere they go. You can find them on street corners, telling people they need to "turn or burn," or on television screaming to all the world that God is going to punish them.

The misbelief that God is angry and vindictive is one you need to deal with as you become Spirit Contemporary. The way to do that is to embrace grace. There's nothing either faithful or contemporary about being judgmental or making people believe God is angry with them. That message is both untrue and ineffective. It drives people away from Jesus. We have a message of grace and forgiveness. God loved the world so much he gave his only Son so that whoever believes in him would not perish but have everlasting life (John 3:16, my paraphrase). Does that sound like an angry God?

Being Spirit Contemporary is knowing who you are in Christ, knowing what Jesus did for us on the cross, and knowing the good things he brings into our lives when we follow him. We can't gain that favor or acceptance through anything *we* do. Jesus qualifies us for it through his death and resurrection, and now we have access to every promise in the Bible. That's grace, pure and simple. It's this message of grace, not judgment, that the world so desperately needs to hear. Will you share it?

HE'S NOT OUT TO GET YOU

Judgmentalism is a misbelief based on a misunderstanding of God's character, and it is directed toward others. A second misbelief based on a misreading of God's nature is *condemnation*. This misbelief isn't directed toward others but at ourselves. To eradicate it, you need to accept the forgiveness God freely offers through faith in Jesus.

Many people believe Holy Spirit watches them day and night, looking to point out the sin in their lives. This is biblically incorrect according to John 16:8–11, which says, "When he comes, he will prove the world to be in the wrong about sin and righteousness and judgment: about sin, because people do not believe in me; about righteousness, because I am going to the Father, where you can see me no longer; and about judgment, because the prince of this world now stands condemned." Any condemnation you feel is not from Holy Spirit. He doesn't convince us as believers of all that's wrong but of all that's right with us because of Jesus! We all experience feelings of guilt when we do wrong. However, lingering, tormenting condemnation is the work of the devil.

How can you tell when the devil is condemning you? When you are plagued by defeating thoughts, when you hate life and yourself, when you feel like a failure with no hope for the future—that's condemnation from the devil. It may seem like those thoughts are coming from God. After all, you know that you have done wrong and you feel bad for it. But God does not condemn.

The devil is called "the accuser of our brothers and sisters" (Revelation 12:10), and he wants you to be defeated, discouraged, and stuck. Holy Spirit convinces us of righteousness and convinces the world they need Jesus! He draws us closer to God rather than making us feel alienated and distant. Holy Spirit is not referred to in the Bible as the judger (or criticizer, faultfinder, nitpicker, condemner, critic). He is your "Comforter, (Counselor, Helper, Intercessor, Advocate, Strengthener, Standby)" (John 14:26, AMPC). He's on your side.

According to Romans 8:1, "Now there is no condemnation for those who belong to Christ Jesus" (NLT). Of course we all have areas in which we need to change. At the same time, know that God is not out to get you. Trust in his love, accept his forgiveness through faith in Jesus, and let his Word change you from the inside out.

To embrace the Spirit Contemporary life, you need to embrace Holy Spirit. To do so, you'll need to confront the limiting misbeliefs that may have taken root in your mind. Most of the common misbeliefs begin with a plausible sounding half truth: *I'm not good enough; I can't; I'm a failure; I can't change what I've always done; God hates sin.* These may have some root in reality. You've probably failed at some point in your life, but that doesn't make you a failure! All of these beliefs, left to themselves, will produce cynicism, failure, judgmentalism, or condemnation.

To free yourself from misbelief, focus on God's truth. If you want to know what God is like, just look at Jesus. You don't find examples in the Bible of Jesus killing people when they did wrong. You don't see him saying, "I can't heal you because you deserve this illness," or "You're not good enough to be saved." Jesus loves people. He loves you. In him, you have health, joy, peace, and so much more.

When we get to know God as he really is, we will become loving, warm, approachable, and easy to be around. Why? Because we are comfortable with God and therefore with who we are in relationship with him. That makes us able to embrace the Spirit Contemporary life.

Holy Spirit knows every aspect of your life, including your future. He knows every intricate detail, and he resides inside of you. Contrary to popular belief, he is not concerned only with your spiritual growth. Holy Spirit wants to "guide you into all truth" in every area of your life (John 16:13, NKJV), which brings us to the topic of our next chapter. You need to align your worldview with the truth—his truth.

8 Shattered Lenses

Imagine you had strapped on a pair of tinted sunglasses as a small child and you've never taken them off. The world, as you see it, is tinted blue. But it doesn't bother you that the whole world is a little blue. In fact, it seems normal and you assume everyone else sees things the same way.

One day you overhear someone talking about the pure white snow that fell the night before. They go into great detail about the brightness of it, how it glistens and sparkles in the sunlight, pure white, like no other color. You wonder what they are talking about because, to you, white doesn't exist—not in the way others see it.

As you think about their words, you remember your sunglasses. You've worn them so long you'd forgotten about them, but as you step out into the cold, crisp morning, you take off the glasses you have worn your entire life. The brightness of the white snow pierces your eyes, causing you to blink back tears. For the first time in your life you experience the sight of pure, untainted, gleaming white snow. You're amazed by this and wonder how this color could have been there all along without your ever seeing it.

The sunglasses in this story are your worldview. Every person has a worldview—a filter through which he or she interprets everything in life. Your worldview colors your perspective on everything. It's a collection of ideas you hold about life and the universe, formed by your personal belief system. Many of these beliefs were formed early in your life, and you may be unaware of them. Some were passed down from parents, teachers, and other people of influence. Others were formed through your experiences.

The white snow in this analogy represents the truth of God's Word. We often think we know the truth, just as you thought you knew what white was before taking off your glasses. But when our view of the truth is colored by an underlying belief system, we completely miss the mark. We either see the truth accurately or we don't. Misperceived truth is error. And Holy Spirit wants to lead us into the whole truth.

If you want to enter the Spirit Contemporary life, you need to know the truth. You need to get your worldview firmly in line with the truth of God's Word.

CLASHING WORLDVIEWS

Your worldview is your foundation for life. Everything you think, and ultimately do, rises from it. Your worldview determines your ability, or lack of ability, to be disciplined. It determines whether or not you are generous, your attitude when you get up in the morning, how you treat your family, and virtually everything else about how you live in the world. Your worldview is a frame for how you live your life.

Not all worldviews are the same, and some worldviews clash. Our society values tolerance, but there are times when your worldview will be in strong opposition to someone else's. Paul, in Colossians 2:8, said, "See to it that no one takes you captive through hollow and deceptive philosophy, which depends on human tradition and the elemental spiritual forces of this world rather than on Christ." In other words, don't let anyone alter your biblical worldview. It's great to be tolerant if that means you accept people no matter what they believe, but if you think tolerance means you have to agree with a false worldview, be intolerant! You can love and accept people while disagreeing with their point of view. Be confident in your source of truth, and find a way to respectfully disagree.

When we give our lives to Christ, we begin the renewal of our minds (see Romans 12:1–2). In other words, our worldview begins to change for the better, to become like Christ's. It would be great if our mind-set changed instantly. Then we would immediately view the world from his perspective. Unfortunately, it doesn't work that way. Over time, and with persistent effort, we come to know and adopt more and more of God's way of thinking. We get a new vision, a new view of our world. We see things differently. It's as if we're getting our first pair of prescription glasses after years of seeing the world through squinting eyes. We put them on and suddenly things become clear. As we begin to see things the way Christ does, we see the truth.

> **Have you ever examined your worldview to understand what it is and where it comes from?**

The Bible presents a very clear worldview that we need to "put on." It is a Spirit Contemporary worldview. What do you value? What's truth? Who decides what's right and wrong? Is it popular opinion? government? church tradition? And where is this world going? Are people intrinsically good? What is the purpose of your life? The answers to questions like these indicate your worldview.

Have you ever examined your worldview to understand what it is and where it comes from? Let's take money as an example of how our worldview can become confused. Many Bible verses relate to prosperity. God has commanded us to "have dominion" over the earth (Genesis 1:28, NKJV). He has told us that we are "above" and "not . . . beneath," "the head and not the tail," that we will "lend to many nations," and he'll make us prosper (Deuteronomy 28:11–13, NKJV). Unfortunately, many wear tinted glasses in this area. Some feel that money is evil and that those who have it are ungodly. Others don't really have a problem with prosperity, yet they feel guilty if they have anything of value.

To be clear, money makes a terrible master. As Paul reminds us, "The *love* of money is the root of all kinds of evil" (1 Timothy 6:10, NLT). We need to seek God first, not money (see Matthew 6:33). So why do we have such trouble with money? Why can't we just focus on God and forget about money?

Financial problems are the second-leading cause of divorce and the number-one cause of stress. Though we do not like to admit it, everything about our lives is affected by money. Jesus knew this, which may be why 20 percent of his teachings concerned money and finances. If he felt that money was important enough to spend a fifth of his time teaching about it, we should pay attention.

For the first hundred years of its history, the church could not be stopped. It was persecuted, but still it exploded. But after roughly three centuries, Christianity was declared the official religion of the Roman Empire. Rather than fighting the church, the world sought to control it. One result was Christians were taught that poverty was godly, and in believing that lie they lost precious opportunities. Today we still struggle with this misbelief, and it still limits our impact. After all, how can we feed and clothe the poor if we are poor ourselves?

To see the truth clearly and recapture a truly biblical worldview, we need to be willing to remove our tinted glasses. God's Word will reveal the areas in our lives that are clouded by misbelief. When we study the Bible, we get "aha moments" when the tint is removed and truth becomes clear. When this happens, it's not that we've discovered a new truth. Truth is eternal. We simply perceive it for the first time because our belief system prevented us from seeing it before. And when we begin to understand what God thinks, our whole world begins to change.

I've seen revelations of truth impact people's lives time and time again, and I know from personal experience that pure, unadulterated truth has the power to change everything.

I remember one time when my realization of God's truth began to change things drastically for me. A couple of months before, I had responded to an emergency call that shook me to the core. My partner and I arrived in the ambulance at the scene of an accident where a car carrying a mom and three kids had crashed into a telephone pole. Just before impact, one of the kids—a little girl about the same age as my oldest daughter—had unbuckled her seat belt. She had been thrown headfirst through the windshield and made contact with the pole. Her little body lay crumpled in the ditch, and although my partner and I tried everything we could to stabilize her, she slowly slipped away.

As the days passed, the memory of this little girl stayed with me. I kept picturing her and the little pigtails she wore in her long brown hair—pigtails just like the ones

I had fixed in my daughter's hair the morning of the accident. Fear began to grip my heart, the fear that I might lose one of my kids.

I began to act differently; I became extremely protective of my children and hard to live with. I began questioning my wife, Sally, every day, sometimes even calling her from work to ask, "Do you know where the kids are? What are they doing?" I would wake up in the middle of the night with my stomach in a knot, to the point where I would get up to check on each one to make sure someone hadn't stolen them out of their beds.

This went on for some time before I finally realized that I had stopped trusting God.

Once I realized that I had allowed fear to take over, I began to study what the Bible had to say to determine the truth. The truth wasn't that I should fear for my kids' lives. The truth was that God had a plan for each of their lives, and His plans are always good (see Jeremiah 29:11). The truth is that his plans for them are so great that I can't even begin to imagine how incredible they are. First Corinthians 2:9–10 says, "What no eye has seen, what no ear has heard, and what no human mind has conceived'—the things God has prepared for those who love him—these are the things that God has revealed to us by [Holy] Spirit."

As I continued to plant God's truth in my heart, that fear that had begun to control my every thought slowly dissipated, day by day, until it was gone. The same can be true for you. As you keep discovering the truth—God's truth in his Word—you will experience the words of Jesus in a whole new way: "Then you will know the truth, and the truth will set you free" (John 8:32).

ETERNITY FOCUSED

If you have a worldview that is not based on God's Word, you will focus on the wrong things. We see that fact in Jesus's conversation with Nicodemus, recorded in John 3.

Nicodemus was a brilliant man. He was a Pharisee who came to Jesus at night so he would not be seen, probably because he didn't want people to know that he had consulted this controversial rabbi from Nazareth. Nicodemus had a lot of questions for Jesus, but Jesus didn't give him a chance to philosophize. Jesus immediately took control of the conversation, saying, "Very truly I tell you, no one can see the kingdom of God unless they are born again" (John 3:3). Understandably, Nicodemus had a hard time wrapping his head around that one.

Notice that Jesus didn't give Nicodemus a chance to ask the wrong questions, bogging down the discussion with his mistaken beliefs about the world. Instead, Jesus directed him to the questions he should be asking.

Your brain is wired to answer every question that comes its way. That's your natural response. And the devil is great at getting you to ask the wrong questions. "Am I really happy in my marriage?" Wrong question. If you go there, you'll become unhappy. "What's wrong with my marriage?" Wrong again. Ask what's right about it. The Enemy came to Eve and posed a question, "Did God really say . . . ?" (Genesis 3:1). Her attention to that one small question altered her destiny, and ours. Having the wrong worldview leads you to ask the wrong questions.

Jesus led Nicodemus to think about the right questions and, through those thoughts, opened up a way of thinking new to him. You see, the problem with Nicodemus was that he was supposed to have been knowledgeable in the things of God, but when God stood before him, Nicodemus couldn't recognize him. Like many today who continue to take on the worldview of religion, he had lost the ability to sense and know God. Jesus engaged Nicodemus's heart by giving him straight truth. This bypassed Nicodemus's faulty belief system and went straight into his spirit.

Then Jesus gave Nicodemus the biggest reality check of all. He said, "Whoever does not believe stands condemned already because they have not believed in the name of God's one and only Son" (John 3:18). With that one statement, Jesus dispatched the mistaken idea that there is any other path to heaven. Jesus is "the way, the truth, and the life" (John 14:6, NKJV).

When you have a chance to speak to nonbelievers about your faith, the only thing standing between their eternity in heaven versus eternity in hell is the fact that they don't know Jesus. When you have that worldview, which is based on God's Word, it changes your focus. You become highly motivated to live the Spirit Contemporary life.

ULTIMATE PURPOSE

When I was about eighteen years old, one of my coworkers was near retirement. One day he collapsed in the men's restroom. Paramedics were called, and as they wheeled him out of the office toward the ambulance, he was fighting for his life. Just as they wheeled the gurney past the time clock, the owner of the business stopped, pulled out this man's timecard, and, with the whole office watching, put it through the time clock. He seemed less concerned about the man's life than he was about ensuring that he didn't have to pay the man more than he had earned.

We live our lives for the most insignificant things. Often we seem to place more value on things that are only temporary while completely ignoring the spiritual world and the life to come. We don't have time for God, because our worldview dictates that career, personal ambition, achievement, entertainment, or any one of a thousand other things are more important. Many times we view our lives through a tinted filter rather than through the eyes of Christ. The Bible tells us to pursue Jesus first; then all other things will be given to us (see Matthew 6:33). Instead, we pursue other things first and make Christ our last priority—or no priority at all. That kind of worldview leads to great pain.

God wants us to experience a satisfying, joyful life. But why? Is it for our own benefit, to make us happy? Yes, he wants us to be blessed and to enjoy our blessings, but there is a purpose for his goodness beyond simply making our lives on earth better. By adopting a biblical worldview, we can see that God's ultimate purpose for us—and the blessings he gives to us—is to bring others to Christ.

Over the years I have read thousands of pages of religious material, and I have never found anything close to the brilliance and the power of the Bible. This incredible book was created over the course of sixteen hundred years, from Moses to John, under the influence of Holy Spirit. There is no greater guide for building a home, a marriage, a family, or a nation. When you determine to live by the truth contained in the pages of the Bible, your life will *not* be more limited and less exciting; it will be *amazing*!

A Spirit Contemporary worldview is a biblical worldview. When you have this Spirit Contemporary view of the world, your priorities center on an eternal purpose.

Seeing the world in this way, God's way, enables you to persevere through difficult times. Life won't always be a picnic, so you need patient endurance. You build this endurance by realizing that if you don't lose heart, you will see the reward of your faith (see Galatians 6:9–10, NKJV). Jesus is building the church, and he is building *you*.

When you line up your worldview with God's, you will see lives transformed. His power is on you to build Jesus's church and see many people come to know this incredible Jesus we serve.

Part 3

FREE TO LIVE

9 Be Who You Is

Becoming Spirit Contemporary isn't difficult. You don't have to alter your personality or change the way you're wired. Becoming Spirit Contemporary is really all about becoming who you already are as a child of God. "Be who you is," as I often say. I know it's bad English, but it's a good point. The problem with many believers today is they're trying to become what they believe they are not.

For example, many people have a desire to be good. Probably everyone does. The problem is many Christians believe they are *not* good people, so they're trying to become something they are convinced they will never be. Talk about a limiting misbelief! Others want to be good spouses, parents, or friends but are certain the traits they need to develop are just beyond their reach. They're working frantically to become something they believe they will never be. That's wrong thinking, and it's a recipe for failure in the Christian life. If you have given your life to Christ, you already *are* everything you will ever need to be.

Let's pause here for a moment, because I'm sure you're wondering how that could be true. I am not saying you become perfect the moment you make the decision to follow Jesus. All of us still have plenty of growing to do. You have thoughts and behaviors that need to change. But there is a critical distinction between your *behavior* as an imperfect person and your *identity* as a child of God. As a believer in Jesus, your identity comes from him. The moment you entered a relationship with him, your entire identity changed. You are no longer a helpless, hopeless sinner (although you may still do things you know are wrong). You are now a righteous, empowered child of God.

Becoming Spirit Contemporary is simply a matter of accepting the identity that is already yours and beginning to live it out in the world.

PRAYING FOR CLAWS

Let me show you what I mean. Imagine one day a man found a newborn lion cub, orphaned on the African savannah. He felt sorry for the little cub, so he brought it home. His poodle had just given birth to pups, so the man added the lion cub to the litter.

As the lion grew, he thought he was a poodle. Why wouldn't he? He was surrounded by dogs who treated him like one of their own. When the man disciplined his dogs, he would roll up a newspaper and give them a slap on the behind. After a couple of years, the lion had grown to full size and weighed over four hundred pounds, yet he still cowered at the sight of the newspaper. The animal didn't know he had the power to break free from the man's control.

One day the lion was walking through the yard when he heard the sound of a full-grown African lion roaring in the wild. He stopped in his tracks, and the hair stood up on the back of his neck. The sound of that lion's roar called out to his true nature. Instantly, he realized he was something larger, greater, more powerful than a dog.

Would this lion need to say to himself, *Wow, I really want to become a lion. I need to change who I am to become what I was meant to be?* Would he need to grow a lion's claws or develop a lion's teeth or a lion's strength? Of course not. He already is a lion. He just needs to believe that. And when he truly accepts his identity, he will begin to act like it.

The same is true for you. You already are a child of God; you just need to realize your true identity as a follower of Christ. According to John 1:12, your faith in Jesus gives you the right to become a child of God. The moment you prayed to invite Jesus into your heart, you took on the identity of a child of God. Although your physical body was born of your mother and father, spiritually you became born of God the moment you decided to follow Jesus. You became a member of his family. Realize that identity, and begin living like the new person God has already created you to be.

Put On Your New Jeans

Being born into God's family gives you a new identity. And with it, you become a new person. You are not who you were or who you sometimes think you still are—a failure, someone who can't get it right, a bad husband, a terrible wife, a lousy kid. You have a new identity—a new self. Being Spirit Contemporary means putting on that new self.

Let me put it this way: in the Middle Ages, sons and daughters of the nobility lived very different lives than the peasants did. They enjoyed all the rights and privileges of being nobles without earning any of it. Their privileges were a birthright and nothing could change that.

Now imagine a king's son had been raised in a peasant's home. He would have lived like a peasant, unaware of his birthright. Though he was a prince, he would only expect to experience the life of a peasant—the hardships, poverty, poor treatment, and terrible living conditions. That's exactly how many of us live today. We are God's children, and he is the "eternal King" (Jeremiah 10:10), but either we don't know or we forget who we are.

Now imagine the king's son somehow discovered his true identity and wanted to return to the palace. Would he have to do something to prove he was worthy of being a prince? No, his identity alone would grant him all the privileges of sonship. In the same way, you don't have to earn your way into God's family. Jesus already did that for you. Like our imaginary prince, you simply have to return to your true place at the King's side. You'll have a few habits to change along the way, just as our prince would have to learn royal manners. That's simply a matter of putting your behavior in line with your identity.

The apostle Paul puts it this way: "Put off your old self, which is being corrupted by its deceitful desires . . . and . . . put on the new self, created to be like God in true righteousness and holiness" (Ephesians 4:22, 24). Elsewhere, he writes, "You're done with that old life. It's like a filthy set of ill-fitting clothes you've stripped off and put in the fire. Now you're dressed in a new wardrobe. Every item of your new way of life is custom-made by the Creator, with his label on it" (Colossians 3:9–10, MSG).

If you wear out your favorite jeans and someone gives you a new pair, they won't do you any good sitting in a drawer. You have to take off the old and put on the new. Paul is basically saying we fling off the old way of living like an old pair of jeans and put on our new life as children of the King. It's as if our change in identity brings with it a new uniform—that is, a new way of living. It's already yours; all you have to do is put it on.

FEEL GOOD ABOUT YOURSELF

If you're like most people, you probably base your self-image on past experiences. If you've failed, you feel like a failure. If you've made poor decisions, you think of yourself as stupid. That's the old way of thinking. When you gave your life to Jesus, he made you entirely new. Your poor choices—made either before or after beginning a relationship with Jesus—do not define you. You need to feel good about yourself or you will never live the life God has for you.

I realize that statement directly contradicts much of the religious teaching you may have heard, which is based on negative motivation. You may have been taught you will burn in hell if you don't follow God's Ten Commandments, so you feel like a failure whenever you mess up. But negative motivation never works, not for long, anyway. Here's why.

One of the most common reasons people distance themselves from God is personal failure. They've been taught that Christians have an advantage in overcoming temptation because Jesus lives inside them, but they still struggle. When they fail to meet the standard they've set for themselves, they become confused. They ask themselves, *If all Christians are supposed to live perfect lives, what's wrong with me?* They conclude either that they are too badly flawed to ever be good or that Christianity simply doesn't work for them.

But that thinking, based on negative motivation, doesn't take into account the full range of our humanity or how persistent the old self can be in keeping a grip on us. Even though you are a brand-new creation, you still have wrong desires. Knowing you are a member of God's family makes you realize it's possible to conquer temptation, but there's no magic wand. We all struggle to keep selfishness at bay.

Trying harder is not the key to change. Screaming at someone to stop what they're doing does nothing to help them change, and berating yourself for failure will never empower you to rise above it. The greatest power for change comes

Trying harder is not the key to change.

from God, and you access that power through faith—by believing Jesus has already made you everything that you want to become. Think better, and you will live better.

How do you gain that better image of yourself? Another version of Colossians 3:10 (NLT) clarifies that you put on the new you "as you learn to know your Creator and become like him." Getting to know God means spending time with him every day. As you do, your self-image will begin to line up with God's image of you. You get to know God better by spending time in his Word every day.

Read the Bible to learn what God says about you. In Jesus, you are God's child (1 John 3:1; Galatians 3:26; 4:6–7; Romans 8:14–15). You are Jesus's friend (John 15:15). You are a citizen of heaven and are seated in heavenly places (Philippians 3:20; Ephesians 2:6). You're also an overcomer and more than a conqueror (1 John 5:4; Romans 8:37). You are loved (John 3:16; Romans 5:8), forgiven (1 John 1:9), strengthened (Philippians 4:13), and full of power, love, and self-control (2 Timothy 1:7; Acts 1:8).

So don't allow yourself to get stuck in condemnation. That negative thinking is sure to keep you stuck in failure. Instead, pick yourself up and keep going. Feed yourself on God's Word, and it will replace your (often mistaken) personal belief systems. As you grow, you will drown out old habits, replace them with positive thoughts and actions, and gain increased confidence in the power Jesus gives you to overcome temptation.

ANTIDOTE FOR FEAR

Becoming Spirit Contemporary means realizing your identity as a child of God, and one aspect of that identity is courage. It takes courage to speak up when Holy Spirit leads you but to do so in a respectful, contemporary way. It takes courage to stand for Christ and to believe for miracles when he leads you to step out. The Spirit Contemporary life is a courageous life. But most of us don't feel all that courageous.

One reason we lack courage is that we accept a high level of stress in our lives. We will hardly ever go through a day without hearing someone say, "I am *so* stressed out right now!" We think this is normal. But stress, especially the intense daily stress that many of us live with, is not normal. It's harmful to us in many ways, and it inhibits us from experiencing the Spirit Contemporary life. Stress is actually fear in disguise. We blame stress on our circumstances, but being stressed out is a direct result of what we believe, not what's happening in our lives.

Stress results from the belief that we have no control over our lives. As a result, we become fearful or anxious about the future, and we experience those negative emotions as stress. But it's not true that we have no control over our lives. Though we can't always control what happens to us, we can always choose our reaction to it. And we can choose our focus. When we surrender the power to choose our reactions, we live in stress and begin to make cowardly choices. We choose to be passive. We choose to take the easy road. We choose to indulge ourselves. We choose to live in the paralysis of self-doubt. In short, we lack the courage to live Spirit-led lives.

Years ago, cowardice wasn't viewed lightly. In the year 1632 during the Thirty Years' War, a battle was fought in Lützen, Germany. During combat, an entire regiment turned and ran. After the battle, all commanders and officers who retreated were arrested, convicted of cowardice, and either beheaded or hanged. Yes, cowardice was once considered a crime, and several men were executed for it: men who had fought bravely for their cause but gave in to a single moment of fear.

I certainly don't condone the execution of those men, but the pendulum seems to have swung to the opposite extreme today. Cowardice is often encouraged. Blame your parents for your failures. Or blame your teachers, your spouse, or your boss. Nothing is your fault. When things get hard, quit. Do whatever it takes to make yourself feel better. Making choices based on fear has become socially acceptable.

As a child of God, you can make a different choice. You can face fear with courage. Although it's tempting to give in to the stress and make choices based on fear, that always turns out worse in the long run. You can choose courage instead, because courage is a choice, not an emotion. Cowards and champions both feel fear, but champions do the right thing regardless of fear—even when that results in their own discomfort.

> **Difficulty and struggles are a part of life, and some days require more courage than others.**

Difficulty and struggles are a part of life, and some days require more courage than others. Many people deal with fear-inducing circumstances every day—walking through losing a loved one, bankruptcy, divorce, unemployment, foreclosure, terminal illness. And each day they stir up the courage to keep going. This is the Spirit Contemporary life: meeting every challenge with the determination to face what's ahead of us rather than making choices based on fear.

We all have made mistakes in this area, so don't feel condemned because of the choices you've made based on fear. Simply resolve to choose courage in the future, and never forget that you have the power to do so. You're not alone! When you chose to follow Jesus, he actually took up residence inside you. Wherever you go, he's there with you, strengthening you and empowering you to face what comes your way.

Much of the fear we face (and therefore the stress we feel) stems from our lack of understanding of who we are in relationship to God. First John 4:18 says that "perfect love drives out fear, because fear has to do with punishment." When we think God is out to punish us, we lack confidence, feel fear, and experience stress in our lives. We can't have confidence because we constantly feel condemned. But Jesus took all our punishment on the cross, so we have no reason to fear God. When we understand that, we experience God's perfect love and peace. That is the antidote for fear and the stress it produces. Knowing God loves us enables us to live with courage.

———

To be Spirit Contemporary, simply be who you already are in Christ. You are an infinitely valuable child of God, regardless of the beliefs or habits you still need to change. Realize your identity as a child of God and live it with confidence.

Remember that your new identity is what gives you the power to really live. Trying to live better on your own strength or willpower only reinforces the bad habits you're fighting against, which brings condemnation and shame. It's a vicious cycle. By surrendering your old self to God and putting on the new nature he has for you, you will find the power to live a new life, the Spirit Contemporary life.

God's Word has much more to say about who you really are. Stop trying to be something that you really don't believe you can ever be, and simply be the new person God has already created in you. Every day say, "I am a child in God's family, and I am destined to do awesome things for him." Then simply be yourself, guided by Holy Spirit. God created you as you are for a purpose. There are people whom I could never connect with or influence, but because of your personality and particular experiences, you're perfect for the job. Never underestimate your influence. You can reach someone in your own way, and you never know whom God is going to bring across your path.

You will become more of who you already are in Christ by getting to know who Jesus really is, which brings us to our next topic. To be Spirit Contemporary, you will need a new, more accurate picture of Jesus.

10 Not Interested in "Your Jesus"

One day I received a frantic phone call from someone to let me know that my brother had been badly hurt and was lying on the ground outside of the caller's house. I sped over to the address I had been given and then jumped out of my car, looking everywhere for his body.

I couldn't see my brother anywhere, but I hardly had time to think about it before a guy burst out the front door of the house with a tire iron in his hand. He came straight at me.

Instantly I recognized him and realized that the story about my brother being hurt was a lie. This guy had threatened me before, and he had tricked me into showing up at his house alone.

As he barreled toward me, I looked him straight in the eye and stood my ground. In a confident voice that communicated I fully understood who had my back, I said, "In the name of Jesus."

I didn't need to say anything more. He stopped dead in his tracks, dropped the tire iron, turned on his heels, and ran full force back into his house.

I turned around, got back into my car, and left.

Jesus lives in you just as he does in me, so you have just as much reason to be confident. In fact, you are empowered to be like Jesus, and he is more powerful than you can imagine!

Many believers have the wrong idea about who Jesus actually is. Because of that, they have difficulty embracing the Spirit Contemporary life. Some depict Jesus as a mild-mannered, sappy guy wearing sandals and a dress who walks around making the peace sign all day. That picture of Jesus is both inaccurate and unhelpful for reaching our world. Jesus certainly did embody love, peace, and patience, but we do him a disservice when we concentrate only on those characteristics and ignore his striking confidence, inspiring leadership, undeterred passion, and unparalleled ability to impact the world.

While many picture Jesus as a timid, flower-power type, John describes the risen Jesus quite differently: "The hair on his head was white like wool, as white as snow, and his eyes were like blazing fire. His feet were like bronze glowing in a furnace, and his voice was like the sound of rushing waters. In his right hand he held seven stars, and coming out of his mouth was a sharp, double-edged sword. His face was like the sun shining in all its brilliance" (Revelation 1:14–16).

I believe Jesus would be kicked out of many churches today because he would be considered un-Christlike! Our ideas of what Jesus is like are often nothing like him. Jesus is not some cute-boyfriend-type with big sad eyes. He is our awe-inspiring, magnificent, powerful, fiercely intense God. You could even describe him as dangerous, not because he is dangerous to others, but because he lived dangerously.

> **I believe Jesus would be kicked out of many churches today because he would be considered un-Christlike!**

Many believers have stopped being in awe of Jesus, and their picture of God is off too. Some see God as a mild-mannered best friend, others as a judgmental busybody, while still others picture him almost like Santa Claus—a jolly guy you don't have to take seriously. What they are doing is reducing God to fit their own categories, but in reality he is beyond our imagination. This amazing God who created the universe is much bigger and more awe inspiring than we can comprehend. And this same God came to us in the person of Jesus Christ.

To be truly Spirit Contemporary, you'll need to put away your preconceived notions about Jesus. He is not a tame, ineffectual wimp. He is the most powerful, radical person ever to walk the planet, so as *Christ*-ians, there should be nothing boring about our lives.

Here are five key aspects of Jesus's character that are often misunderstood by believers today. When you begin to truly understand who Jesus is, you'll want to join this incredible adventure called the Spirit Contemporary life.

POWERFUL

Jesus said, "Blessed are the meek, for they will inherit the earth" (Matthew 5:5), and that word "meek" really trips people up. When Jesus used that word, he didn't mean he or his followers would be timid, soft spoken, and wimpy. That's the definition we often assign to the word *meek,* so we conclude we have to be shy, unassuming, and fearful of confrontation in order to please God. That misunderstanding has created a culture in the church that is repulsive to strong men and women. When we portray Jesus this way, we don't attract people to him. They aren't interested in becoming powerless, emotionally weak people who allow others to take advantage of them and their families. The next generation doesn't want to serve a Lord who is too powerless to make a difference in their lives and in the world. We have to stop toning Jesus down and start seeing him as he really is.

Churches that portray a distorted picture of Jesus form cultures that discourage confidence and strength because they mistake those traits for pride. I encountered this many times as a younger Christian, and I thought that's the way it was supposed to be. Then I discovered the true meaning of the word *meek,* and it set me free to see the real Jesus.

In the language of the Bible, the word we translate as "meek" is the same word used to describe war-horses. The Greek word is *praus,* which means "power under control." This word was used to describe a horse that was trained to obey instantly and absolutely, no matter how loud and brutal the battle. When Greek soldiers had trained a horse to be controlled by nothing more than a touch from its rider, they called that horse *praus*. With only a nudge of the knee or a tug of the reins by the rider, the horse responded immediately.

Although these animals were tremendously powerful, having the ability to propel their thousand-pound frames to speeds over thirty-five miles per hour, their power was under complete control. And while they may have been gentle to their riders, they were fierce in battle. They would paw at the ground in anticipation, unafraid of the thundering sounds of the enemy bashing swords and lances against shields in an effort to intimidate. This type of horse seemed to devour the ground with fierceness and rage and couldn't stand still when it heard the call to battle (see Job 39:19–25).

Jesus was this kind of meek: power under control. He certainly wasn't timid or afraid of conflict. He spoke to crowds of thousands and had no problem standing up to powerful religious leaders. He walked the earth with all the power of Holy Spirit in him—healing the sick and raising people from the dead. Boring? Not a chance. And Jesus was passionate. He had such incredible love and unconditional acceptance for those around him that people flocked to him by the thousands. He respected people and in return gained their respect.

In fact, he was loved by many, especially those who were rejected by the rest of society, like tax collectors and prostitutes. Jesus understood the needs of people and met them there. Even at the wedding where he performed his first miracle, Jesus seems to have understood the embarrassment the host would suffer at running out of wine. In something as seemingly insignificant as that, he met people where they were and filled their needs without judgment.

At the same time, Jesus didn't shrink back from confronting people's behavior when necessary. He didn't seem to worry about people leaving him, because he had confidence that he was doing Father's will. He was perfectly led by Holy Spirit, and he was powerfully attractive to people. He was Spirit Contemporary.

Believers today think being meek means not rocking the boat. This misbelief about Jesus's character causes many of his current followers to be people pleasers, always worried about what others think. They run around like chickens with their heads chopped off, trying to get people to like them. Meanwhile, many people, especially those with a strong sense of self-worth, are turned off by this approach to faith. They interpret this overconcern and the accompanying mild-mannered, inoffensive, people-pleasing behavior as signs of weakness. Being Spirit Contemporary isn't about pleasing people so they will like you. It's about being so confident, strong, and secure in your identity as a child of God that people notice the difference in your life and are *attracted* to you as you direct them toward Jesus.

If you're wearing yourself out trying to get everyone to like you, you're not being Christlike. That approach to the Christian faith says more about your own insecurities and misbeliefs than about Jesus, and the way to deal with them is to understand who Jesus really is and who you are in him. Derive your self-worth from your relationship with God; then you will develop an attractive sense of self-confidence.

People are attracted to warriors who serve the King of kings. They respond to confident believers who respect other people.

LOVING

Another word that has been misunderstood by Christians over the years is *love*. Our misunderstanding of the true meaning of *love* has made us appear pathetic to the world. Jesus taught us to love our neighbors, and most people assume he was talking about a sappy, sentimental, emotional feeling. They think this means we have to gush over people and act sweet and cute toward them in order to love them. Many people, especially men, don't respect or respond to this kind of behavior. But that's not at all what Jesus meant when he used the word *love*.

One problem we face is that we represent several ideas with the single English word *love*. We usually think of love in sentimental, even romantic, terms. That leads us to the conclusion that to love others is to have warm feelings toward them and act sweet all the time. But the concept of love is much broader than that. To love people, as Jesus used the term, means to *value* them.

I can walk into a room and maintain my strong, confident composure, while demonstrating I value each person tremendously. This has nothing to do with my personal feelings or the emotions I may feel toward them. There is nothing sappy about this aspect of love. Because I know who I am in Christ and am acutely aware of the power that backs me through Holy Spirit, I can look every person in the eye and communicate that I value them for who they are, just as they are. That's a powerful kind of love!

CONFIDENT

Humility is another aspect of Jesus's character that is often misunderstood. Many Christians have been taught that to have humility, you have to think very little of yourself. We think we should duck compliments and say things like "I'm just a sinner saved by grace," honestly believing we are worth nothing either to other people or to God. Maybe we're trying to act on Jesus's teaching that "the first will be last" (Matthew 20:16), but our constant self-deprecation comes across as weakness to the world.

The problem is we misunderstand Romans 12:3, which warns us to "not think of [ourselves] more highly than [we] ought." But that verse is speaking about your ability, not your worth as a person. It's true that you shouldn't exaggerate your ability. Don't tell a group of rookie mountain climbers you can lead them on an expedition if you've never climbed a rock. You're going to get yourself and everyone else killed! We need to be honest about what we can and can't do.

Yet when it comes to your personal sense of worth, remember these two things. First, you can think as highly of yourself as you want as long as you give God all the credit. Second, make sure you always think of others as even greater than yourself. You can be confident in yourself and your God-given abilities; just direct the credit to God, and give others the respect they deserve. Then there will no room for arrogance or pride in you.

God doesn't want you to think you're worthless. That doesn't please him. God wants you to realize you can be the best. Many Christians may have a real problem with that statement because they have been taught that to follow Christ is to think little of themselves. It is absolutely true that "God opposes the proud but shows favor to the humble" (James 4:6), which is why you absolutely should not think you are better than everyone else. However, God does want you to be the very best you can be.

Believing you are capable of anything God asks you to do is not pride; it's faith. And the truth is that this confidence, which stems from who you are in Christ, is incredibly attractive to others. Jesus had this confidence. He was the first Spirit Contemporary man. He was full of power, wisdom, and divine insight. He worked miracles, and he taught profound spiritual truths. Yet Jesus did all this in a way that was contemporary in regard to the culture and times in which he lived. He was culturally relevant and filled with Holy Spirit's power, and people flocked to him.

OBEDIENT

Let's return to the concept of meekness for a moment. Remember that the true meaning of *meekness* is "strength under control." One way that played out in the life of Jesus was that he was fully obedient to God's will, totally unafraid and eager to do what needed to be done. Those who are like Christ are completely and instantly responsive to God's will.

You can be strong, powerful, and courageous and still be like Jesus. In fact, you really have to be! Meekness is neither a feminine nor a masculine quality. It is being instantly obedient to the Master, and sometimes he asks us to do tough things. Today many believers are suffering for their faith in Jesus, and some are sacrificing their lives. That kind of obedience does not come from weakness or timidity. Meek is powerful. Moses was described as the meekest person "upon the face of the earth," but he was no pushover (Numbers 12:3, KJV). He is one of our strongest examples of godly leadership. If Moses was meek yet confronted Pharaoh, the most powerful ruler on the earth at the time, commanding him to release the Hebrew people from slavery, then *meekness* and *confidence* are clearly not opposites.

Are you willing to trust God no matter what? Are you ready to obey him immediately and completely, no matter the cost? It takes tremendous strength to say yes to those questions—*strength under control.* That's meekness.

COMPASSIONATE

When Jesus walked the earth, people followed him because he lived with incredible power. There was nothing he couldn't do. He was ready for all situations, never thrown off balance, never at a loss for words, never confused. He was perfectly led by Holy Spirit, so he dealt with every situation with wisdom and strength.

Today, some Christians are good at being contemporary but have lost touch with Holy Spirit. They have rapport with people but no ability to work with or hear from God's Spirit. They have no power. Without Holy Spirit, there are no life-changing transformations and no miracles. Without that power, there is nothing to offer hurting, lost people who are asking, "Can somebody help me?"

We pass these hurting people every day, often without noticing. When we do notice, we are just as likely to be judgmental of them as to reach out. That's because, without Holy Spirit's power, we have nothing to offer them.

Here's a confession: I once looked at needy people in that judgmental way. I had to stop thinking that people who do bad things or wind up in bad circumstances are bad people. Religion throws that kind of thinking at us, but that's not how Jesus thought about people. He was able to sympathize with their weaknesses because he had been tempted in every way and yet was without sin (see Hebrews 4:15). He doesn't judge people who have failed. He understands their brokenness—and he has the power to help.

When we are Spirit Contemporary, we are strong and confident. Our words are "like apples of gold in settings of silver" (Proverbs 25:11). We let Holy Spirit lead us into all truth and guide us into every adventure. We speak and act in a way that reveals the heart of Jesus, and people will fall in love with the Jesus they see in us.

At the same time, we develop a powerful edge that refuses to shrink back. Jesus had this edge. He was completely obedient to Holy Spirit, which required incredible courage and resolve, and he was full of confidence. God's greatness is unbelievable. He is the all-powerful Creator of the universe! He has no need to be mean or judgmental, but he also isn't a benign Santa Claus. He is a good, loving Father who has the power to transform the lives of broken people.

Some people have a false notion of the Christian life based on misbeliefs about the character of Jesus. Others believe church should be boring because they mistake boredom for reverence. Although Jesus does want us to be in awe of our heavenly Father and to live lives that are filled with peace and joy, we can't forget we're here for a purpose, and that purpose is to take part in his great big, exciting adventure to transform the world. The truth is Jesus's life was anything but boring. He was a strong, courageous, confident leader who followed his Father's will instantly and completely. In the same way, this Spirit Contemporary life he's calling us to live is also filled with adrenaline and adventure.

It's also filled with significance. Fulfilling Jesus's purpose for our lives is the most important thing we can do on this planet! It's absolutely incredible to think that our actions actually help to determine how many people make heaven their home for eternity. Don't ever forget that you are included in this mission. This grand, phe-

> **The truth is Jesus's life was anything but boring.**

nomenal purpose for our lives is just as real as the fact that we have his grace and that we're forgiven, and when it comes to the big picture, you play a vital role!

God's plans for us are absolutely huge, greater than you can imagine. The apostle Paul quoted Isaiah in saying, "No eye has seen, no ear has heard, and no mind has imagined what God has prepared for those who love him" (1 Corinthians 2:9, NLT), and he said that God is "able to do immeasurably more than all we ask or imagine, according to his power that is at work within us" (Ephesians 3:20). According to Psalm 139:13, God formed every aspect of your being. He placed gifts and abilities inside you so you could achieve amazing things in this lifetime.

Be Spirit Contemporary. Live an amazingly huge life, with as much adventure, power, and greatness as you want. After all, Jesus came to give you this kind of life. He said, "I came that they may have *and* enjoy life, and have it in abundance (to the full, till it overflows)" (John 10:10, AMPC). He wants you to live a big life! As you keep listening to Holy Spirit and serving others with the gifts and abilities he has placed in you, you are going to discover this life—the life he died to give you. And this brings us to the topic of our next chapter. When it comes to learning how to listen to Holy Spirit and serve others, Jesus has provided us with the very best example to follow.

11   Jesus Came to End Religion

"I don't like organized religion." That's the most common thing I hear when I tell people I'm a pastor. I always respond, "Me neither," which really confuses people. They can't understand how a pastor could dislike religion, but it's true. There's nothing about religion I enjoy.

You see, Christianity isn't religion. Religion is a systematic approach to life that burdens people. It weighs them down with rules they need to follow and rituals they need to perform in order to please God. Religion assumes you have to earn your way into God's good graces, which is actually impossible. You never have been and never will be good enough to earn a place in heaven, which is why religion is so exhausting, frustrating, and hopeless.

Jesus didn't come to earth to start another religion. He made that clear in Matthew 11:28–30 when he said, "Are you tired? Worn out? Burned out on religion? Come to me. Get away with me and you'll recover your life. I'll show you how to take a real rest. Walk with me and work with me—watch how I do it. Learn the unforced rhythms of grace. I won't lay anything heavy or ill-fitting on you. Keep company with me and you'll learn to live freely and lightly" (MSG).

Jesus came to free us from the futility of religion and offer us something so much better—a real relationship with God. Through that relationship, we can rest. We can learn what grace really is. We can live *freely* and *lightly*.

One look at Jesus's life shows he was fully connected to his heavenly Father. Jesus often slipped away by himself to spend time with his Father in prayer (see Matthew 14:23; Mark 1:35; Luke 5:16; 6:12). Jesus knew that his purpose and the messages he shared weren't his own (see John 12:49); he was being led by his Father, by Holy Spirit (see Matthew 4:1; Luke 2:27; 4:1). In other words, Jesus grew closer to his Father throughout his lifetime.

Luke 2:52 states this directly: "Jesus grew in wisdom and in stature and in favor with God and all the people" (NLT). Jesus grew in relationship with God the Father, and as we are in a relationship with Jesus, we do too. It's not about following rules or keeping traditions. Our life in him is based on growing in this new relationship with God.

Look at the last part of this verse, which says Jesus grew in favor with "all the people." What does that mean? When you think about it from a business perspective, growing in favor with people means building rapport and gaining trust. This has to be done genuinely. Gaining the respect of others to affect their decisions for your own benefit is manipulation. Gaining trust in order to benefit them is called influence.

From a relational perspective, growing in favor with people involves compassion. That kind of favor is created by listening and loving. It means being patient and kind and finding ways to honor others and look out for their interests.

The fact that Jesus grew in favor with both God and others shows he was concerned with more than his own spiritual well-being. He wanted to also influence others and connect them with God. Growing in favor with others was a priority for Jesus, yet most churches ignore this area of growth. They spiritualize everything they do, reducing their mission in the world to a small part of Luke 2:52—growing in favor with God. But God is interested in all aspects of your life, including your relationships with others. The Spirit Contemporary life is first about growing in favor with God through your connection with Holy Spirit. Second, and just as important, it is about growing your influence with those around you, just as Jesus did. That makes him our best example of the Spirit Contemporary life. Let's flesh that out a little more.

FOUR AREAS OF GROWTH

Social scientists measure a person's growth in four areas of intelligence. They are the *intelligence quotient* (IQ), *spiritual quotient* (SQ), *adversity quotient* (AQ), and *emotional quotient* (EQ).

You've likely heard of IQ, which measures aptitude for mental processes, such as reading comprehension and problem solving. But that's only one aspect of your intelligence.

SQ is the effort you put into your relationship with God and your progress in that endeavor. This includes your desire to learn God's Word, the ability to sense when he is leading you, and your willingness to act on his direction for your life.

AQ is a measurement of your ability to persevere. People with a high AQ have a high tolerance for adversity and will keep going even when times are tough.

Finally, EQ is the measure of your ability to gauge and respond appropriately to the emotions of others. Your EQ, sometimes called *emotional intelligence,* affects your ability to understand and work with people. This includes your ability to control your own emotions as well as your ability to read social cues.

You may have met people who have a very high IQ but a low EQ. They are brilliant intellectually, but no one likes to be around them because they lack social skills. Other people struggle with school and exams but are absolute bulldogs when it comes to problem solving. They can tolerate just about any level of conflict when they are zeroed in on a goal. The truth is that we all have different strengths in each of these areas, but it's also true that we can grow in all four quotients.

Experts used to think that your IQ was fixed, but it's been proven you can increase it. You can also increase your AQ by developing a tolerance for adversity. You can grow closer to God, increasing your SQ. And you can increase your EQ—your ability to connect with people—which is just another way of saying that you can learn to become more contemporary.

Jesus had each of these quotients in perfect balance. He had a great relationship with God, yet he also had the ability to draw people to himself. He was contemporary yet powerfully filled with Spirit. Miracles happened everywhere he went, yet he was able to make people feel at ease, loved, and forgiven. He continually grew in favor with God (Spirit) and others (contemporary). And he wasn't alone. Every great leader in the Bible functioned that way. They were closely connected to God and highly influential with others. In that sense, being Spirit Contemporary is nothing new.

SPIRIT CONTEMPORARY IN THE BIBLE

Spirit Contemporary is not a new concept. It may be a new term, but it's not a new idea. In the Bible we see that all of God's great leaders were growing both their relationship with him and their ability to influence others by showing respect, adapting to their surroundings, and leading with excellence and passion. They all had high SQ and high EQ.

The Spirit Contemporary leaders in the New Testament were filled with Holy Spirit, but the leaders we read about in the Old Testament were Spirit Contemporary too, in a different way. Holy Spirit didn't reside inside them because Jesus hadn't yet made that possible, but Holy Spirit still communicated with them in powerful ways. You could say he was with them but not in them. Here are just a few examples of Spirit Contemporary leaders in the Bible.

Moses

Moses was raised in Pharaoh's palace and spent forty years learning Egyptian culture. That was no accident. God orchestrated Moses's upbringing so he would understand Egyptian life and gain skills he would need later. Given his upbringing, he would have studied military tactics and maneuvers, so when it came time for him to lead more than two million people through harsh desert conditions, he knew what to do. God spoke directly to Moses, and Moses had a firm grasp on the times in which he lived. That's the very definition of Spirit Contemporary.

Esther

Esther went through very thorough training as a concubine of the king and "won the favor of everyone who saw her" (Esther 2:15). Esther also won the favor of the king, so much so that he fell in love with her and made her his queen. This put Esther in a prime position of influence, and she was also open to the leading of God. As a result, she was able to influence the king, but only because she had learned how to best approach him. She understood the protocol to follow in approaching the king to best present her case. She used wisdom and faith. That's Spirit Contemporary in action.

Daniel

Daniel was a captive in Babylon, where he learned the culture, language, and ways of the land. But he didn't compromise what he believed. When Daniel was offered the king's food, he chose vegetables and water instead, refusing to eat foods that were contrary to the law God had established.

Later, when a group of jealous officials set Daniel up by creating a law that forbade prayer for thirty days, Daniel kept on praying. He was thrown into the lions' den for disobeying the law, but God protected him, and because Daniel had gained so much influence and the king liked him so much, the king couldn't eat or sleep that night. He rushed to the lions' den in the morning to see what had happened and found Daniel miraculously untouched.

Daniel's influence, coupled with God's miraculous power in his life, caused that king to begin serving God. Actually, he wrote a new law—not one forbidding worship but one that actually *required* people to worship God!

Paul

Paul demonstrates the Spirit Contemporary life in the New Testament. He was trained in the best Jewish schools and understood the culture, so he was well positioned to influence the religious leaders in Jerusalem. When he reached out to them, he spoke their language, respected their laws, and dressed and acted as they did.

When Paul visited Athens, a center of Greek culture, he met with the intellectuals of the city on Mars Hill. There, rather than citing Jewish law as he had done with the religious leaders in Jerusalem, he connected with them by citing their poets and philosophers. He started the conversation by showing them respect, quoting from an inscription he had observed in the city (see Acts 17:16–23).

Paul adapted his approach based on the context. Imagine how much time Paul must have spent studying culture. He could quote the Cretan poet Epimenides from the sixth century BC (see verse 28) as easily as the Jewish Torah or the rabbis of Jerusalem. Paul summed up his Spirit Contemporary attitude in 1 Corinthians 9:19–23, saying,

> Though I am free and belong to no one, I have made myself a slave to everyone, to win as many as possible. To the Jews I became like a Jew, to win the Jews. To those under the law I became like one under the law (though I myself am not under the law), so as to win those under the law. To those not having the law I became like one not having the law (though I am not free from God's law but am under Christ's law), so as to win those not having the law. To the weak I became weak, to win the weak. I have become all things to all people so that by all possible means I might save some. I do all this for the sake of the gospel, that I may share in its blessings.

Everything Paul did was done for the sake of the gospel (Spirit), and he was willing to go to any length to communicate with others (contemporary). Today's Spirit Contemporary equivalent of Paul's speech on Mars Hill might be to quote from a popular movie or song when telling people about Jesus. But the Spirit Contemporary life involves even more than communication techniques like that. Paul took the time to understand the people he was talking with, and that's what being Spirit Contemporary is all about.

SANTA IN CHURCH

Sally and I are inspired by these biblical examples of Spirit Contemporary in action— inspired to see our church from the perspective of a first-time guest. We challenge our team to filter everything we do through the eyes of someone who has never set foot in church before and to modify things as needed to make newcomers comfortable. At Christmastime, we have someone dress up as Santa Claus because that's what unchurched people often think of when they think of Christmas. My messages teach the real reason for the season of course, but having Santa walk the hallways is a fun way to help people who are unfamiliar with church to feel at home.

The first time we did this, a member of our church approached me after a service to tell me he had a problem with Santa being in church. I understood his reasons, and I agree that we should never take the focus away from Jesus. But considering the fact that every other aspect of the service points to Jesus—from worship songs to videos, skits, and the message—having Santa in the hallway is not a big distraction. When I asked that church member how having Santa around would have appeared to an unchurched family who attended for the first time, he realized it would have shown them how comfortable and inviting our church really is.

Paul was willing to be "all things to all people" (1 Corinthians 9:22). Are you willing to change your approach to gain an opportunity to be heard? Will you bend on a few man-made traditions if that's what it takes to reach more people for Christ?

Here's another example of how our good intentions can actually communicate the wrong message, while being Spirit Contemporary opens the door to reaching people. On Halloween, many Christians shut off their porch lights and refuse to take part in the trick-or-treating. I understand their objection, and I admire their resolve. But what are they really accomplishing? Does that action really help lead people to Jesus?

Our family decided a long time ago to join the party. We want to be open and approachable to the people on our street, and we won't be if we're seen as the stingy, uptight Christian family.

You and I understand the history behind Halloween, but are the little kids who go door to door all decked out in costumes reading into it that deeply? I don't think so. They're just looking for a friendly face and a bit of generosity. I wonder what would happen if more Christians used this holiday as an opportunity to meet neighbors and make the neighborhood kids feel welcome.

THROUGH THEIR EYES

Being Spirit Contemporary involves growing in favor with your neighbors by doing what a psychologist might call raising your EQ. This means understanding the culture in which you live, listening carefully to people, meeting them where they are, and responding appropriately for the situation. Let me give you an example.

A couple years ago, I had lunch with a man I know in a city I frequently visit. I hadn't shared much about my faith with him yet, but he had been watching me on TV. At one point he asked me, "Leon, can I ask you a question? Do you pray in the Spirit?"

I paused for a second to think about what this man was really asking. He had probably picked up some ill-informed ideas about what it means to pray in the Spirit, and he may have been thinking, *Are you one of those weird Christians I've heard so much about?* So I was careful in my response. When I said, "No, I don't pray that way, not in the way you're thinking," I saw him visibly relax. Then I explained prayer to him in a way that made sense in his world. I said, "There's something special I'd like to share with you. You know how Tibetan monks chant certain words to lower their heart rates? And in yoga, people use words to calm the mind? Well, in the Bible we learn that there's a language for believers that has a similar effect, and it can help you to experience God."

"Whoa," he said, "that sounds really cool!" Then we went on with our conversation.

I realize that's not exactly how a theologian or Bible scholar would explain praying in the Spirit. But I wasn't speaking to a theologian. I was speaking to someone who had been turned off by what he considered an odd practice among Christians. I wasn't interested in getting into a debate. I just wanted to see things from his point of view and challenge his preconceived notions in an intriguing way. That's Spirit Contemporary in action.

> **When you begin to think like your neighbors, you will see things from their point of view.**

When you begin to think like your neighbors, you will see things from their point of view. When you drop the Christian jargon and relate to them in an honest, open way, right where they are, you will gain favor or trust. And you will open the door to sharing your faith in a powerful yet nonthreatening way.

I'm not saying you have to celebrate Halloween to be Spirit Contemporary; just stop judging people who do! If the apostle Paul could quote a hymn to Zeus in order to gain the respect of his hearers and bring them to Christ, if he could "become all things to all people [in order to] save some" (1 Corinthians 9:22), then we can certainly dress up like Santa or hand out candy on October 31 to reach the same end. Put aside your worries about what other Christians might think long enough to see through the eyes of people who don't know Jesus. When you do, you'll understand their thinking and their needs and gain their respect in the process.

Jesus is our perfect example. When he walked the earth, he was powerfully led and empowered by Holy Spirit, and he was perfectly able to connect with the people of his day. He listened to them. He had a welcoming presence. He was never put off by people, no matter how troubled or far from God they were. In fact, the least churchy people seemed to love Jesus most. Jesus had favor with God and with others. As you live the Spirit Contemporary life, you will too.

Part 4

ALL SPIRIT

12   Connecting with Holy Spirit

Often, when people try to understand Spirit Contemporary, they focus mostly on what it means to be "contemporary." After all, we all want to relate the gospel to the world we live in. But Spirit Contemporary begins with *Spirit*. Jesus grew in favor with God, which means we need to as well. That involves learning God's ways and sensing his presence. We all crave this connection, and if the church doesn't teach us how to develop it, we'll look for it elsewhere.

Any of us can get to know Holy Spirit better and understand him more. He wants to guide you into all truth and direct your life, but you do need to develop your relationship with him. Unfortunately, many believers have misconceptions about what it means to be led and empowered by Holy Spirit. They think it has to be dramatic or sensationalized to be real, and that misconception is costing us dearly.

In reality, Holy Spirit deals with us in ways that are normal and natural. It isn't complicated at all. In fact, it can be as easy as breathing.

CHOOSE CAREFULLY

Many people are afraid of being led by Holy Spirit because they've seen people act strangely, claiming Holy Spirit had taken over their bodies to make them act out of control. These people think you have to fall on the floor when Holy Spirit fills you with his power or act in other bizarre ways. It is true *some* people seem to authentically fall to the ground when overcome with Spirit's presence (although it's never happened to me), but I've also seen many take a backward glance before falling. The fact that they look to be sure someone is there to catch them shows they are consciously choosing to fall. They're in control.

Obviously in these cases their reactions were just that—*their* reactions. Choice was involved. In fact, most of the "spiritual" events claimed by these extreme types are not Holy Spirit's doing at all. They are conscious choices people make in response to Holy Spirit's presence. In other words, they act strangely because they choose to!

In reality, people's reactions to Holy Spirit's work are as varied as the people themselves. There is no right way to respond to something wonderful in your life. For example, suppose I approach three people who are having financial trouble and offer each of them a hundred thousand dollars.

The first person is a mom who couldn't afford to take her very sick child to an expensive clinic for medical help—until now. Tears immediately stream down her cheeks.

The second person had been saving for years to take his family on a trip to Disney World but lost everything in a bad business deal. When he sees the money, he's unable to contain his excitement. He jumps onto the nearest chair and starts to whoop and holler.

The third person had just lost his job and was about to lose his house. He can't believe the timing of this incredible gift. In response, he sinks into a chair and stares, open mouthed, with an expression of disbelief.

You might see tears, shouting, or a blank look, all in response to the same event, and each one would be normal for the person in question. At the same time, a fourth person could receive the same gift and respond in yet a different way. Would anyone say, "That person didn't really receive the gift," or "That person must not have really understood it," just because that person's immediate reaction didn't match the others'? Of course not. There isn't just one way to respond to an incredible, generous, life-changing gift.

The same is true with the wonderful gifts Holy Spirit brings us, such as healing, financial help, peace, and joy. People respond to them in different ways because, well, people are different. You don't need to worry that Holy Spirit will make you behave in some strange way that is totally out of character for you.

I have seen people touched by God in magnificent ways, and I have seen many reactions. Some were overcome with joy as their depression lifted after years of suffering. Others were quietly grateful after being healed of illnesses that had caused tremendous pain. Their reactions were night-and-day different in response to the work of the same God. And why wouldn't they be? People are different, after all.

Some have confused the work of Holy Spirit with the outward reaction to that work. One is a gift from God, the other is a personal response to the gift. People may have all kinds of emotional and physical reactions to Holy Spirit's power. That doesn't mean that the way one person reacts is a pattern for all others. In fact, there are too many cases where people who make dramatic or showy responses to Holy Spirit do so because they are looking for attention. That's tragic because God is magnificent enough on his own; we don't need to dress up our interactions with him.

I make such a point of this because these overdone displays have turned off many people from having a relationship with Christ. Intelligent, level-headed people see through those acts and keep walking. Who could blame them? The truth is God can and does operate in all his power in our lives but in a way that is normal and natural for each individual. He is not limited to our preconceived notions of what his power should look like.

WHO'S LOOKING THROUGH THE GLASS?

Even in what seems like extreme circumstances, Holy Spirit can work through us normally and naturally. I discovered this one day when I was called to the police station to help out with what they said was a really unique situation.

When I entered the station, an officer led me toward the holding rooms. Instantly, I noticed a young man behind a wall of glass who looked like he had completely lost his mind. He was screaming and thrashing around, trying to get free of the three officers who were holding him down.

The officer in charge explained that they had done everything they could think of to calm him without success and had resorted to trying to restrain him because they were afraid he would injure himself if they didn't. Then he filled me in on the story.

This man and a group of his family members had been at home just outside the city limits, drinking and doing drugs. During a heated argument over a card game, he had become so angry that he grabbed a rifle, pointed it at his family, and fired several shots in their direction. He then ran out into the yard and put the barrel in his mouth. Thankfully, it was a long rifle so he couldn't reach the trigger, and a family member was able to wrestle him down before he managed to hurt himself.

Miraculously, no one had been injured in the gunfire. He had missed every person in the room. But in his agitated state of mind, he was convinced that he had killed his entire family. Once in custody, he had mentioned God several times, which prompted the officers to call me. They were hoping I could get through to him and convince him that his family was okay.

I prayed a silent *Lord, what do I do here?* prayer, and a sense of peace flooded over me. I then asked the officer in charge to remove the three others who were trying to restrain the man so I could go in and talk to him.

"Are you crazy?" he replied. "Three trained officers can hardly contain this guy. There's no telling what he'll do to you!" After some convincing, assuring him that they could rush in at the first sign of trouble, he finally agreed.

The officers filed out, and as I walked in, the young man was on the edge of his chair like a tiger ready to pounce. Saliva dripped from his chin, and he was hissing, snarling, and shouting obscenities. Books I had read about demonology came to mind. Some had advised that the way to deal with people in this condition was to shout "Name yourself, you evil spirit!" Others insisted that you need to fast and pray before dealing with a situation like this. None of it made sense to me in that moment, but I could recognize God's peace, and I trusted him to make something happen. I knew Holy Spirit would take charge if I stayed open to him.

> I prayed a silent *Lord, what do I do here?* prayer, and a sense of peace flooded over me.

As I continued to walk toward the man, I felt an unconditional love for him. I said, "It's going to be okay," and I could see the visible effect of those words on his demeanor. It was like peace had just flooded the room. He became calm, and I was able to tell him that his family was alive. He started to cry and thank God.

I then asked if he could sense the peace that entered the room, and he said he could. "That's because Jesus is in me," I said. "You're sensing his presence." I asked if he wanted to have Jesus in him too, so that that peace would remain when I left the room. He nodded. "When you give your life to him," I said, "you'll be free from all the wrong you've done in God's eyes. You'll be completely forgiven."

We prayed a simple prayer together as he gave his life to Jesus, and it was like a burden he had been carrying for a long time lifted. We talked for a while about what he faced in the judicial system as a consequence of his actions, but I assured him that God would never leave him; the peace he felt would never leave him if he stayed connected to Jesus.

Suddenly a funny feeling came over me. I had been so focused on this man, I'd forgotten where I was. I turned around to see six officers staring wide-eyed through the glass. Three officers had barely been able to contain him, so they couldn't believe one guy had walked into that room alone and calmed the situation. Of course I didn't do it; it was Holy Spirit!

I didn't need to engage in strange and complicated tactics of spiritual warfare in order to see Holy Spirit work. He did so in a loving, contemporary, and very normal way with this hurting young man.

God wants to use you too, just as you are, wherever you are. No strange behaviors are required. All you need is the desire to work with Holy Spirit in the circumstances of your everyday life, and he wants to do so in such a normal, natural way. This brings us to the topic of the next chapter. You see, sometimes Holy Spirit's leading is as natural as a gut feeling.

13 Gut Feelings

Holy Spirit already knows how to reach every culture and generation. He knows the words to use, the actions to take, when to speak, and when to stay quiet. He is able to get through to the hurting heart of any person in any situation. That makes it imperative for us to grow in favor with God; we need to learn how to hear Holy Spirit's voice and sense his leading. When we follow Holy Spirit's direction, we don't have to try hard to become contemporary—we will be.

You have a deep desire to be led by Holy Spirit, and that longing comes from God. He has designed you to lean on him for direction, and he has made a way for you to receive that direction every day. Unfortunately, many have been misled about how we hear from God. They sit around waiting for a message written across the sky, a word of prophecy from another believer, a remarkable opportunity that has to be an open door from God, or some supernatural sign.

God could choose to speak to you in any of those ways, but the truth is he probably won't. Holy Spirit's leading usually doesn't come from some external source such as a sign or miracle. It usually comes from within.

Honestly, most of the time when people share with me something they believe to be Holy Spirit's leading, it turns out they are way off. When I was dating Sally, for example, someone said God told them she wasn't right for me. If I had been looking for some sign from God from the outside, I might have been misled by that. I can assure you after years of happy marriage that that person was dead wrong. Fortunately, I listened to Holy Spirit's leading on my own and made the best choice of my life!

On several other occasions when people have spoken into my life, I'm confident that what they shared was from God. But it's important to be discerning. People are often guided by their own thoughts and feelings rather than by Holy Spirit. Besides, God doesn't want us to rely primarily on others to receive direction. He wants us to be able to hear from him directly. Living the Spirit Contemporary life involves learning to identify and trust your internal sense of Holy Spirit's leading.

Spinning Hubcaps

Holy Spirit will lead you in a very personal way. Sometimes that leading comes through the Word, as Holy Spirit brings Bible verses to mind when you're going about your day. But he also leads you in another way, one that comes very naturally. Proverbs 20:27 says, "The spirit of man is the candle of the LORD, searching all the inward parts of the belly" (KJV). In other words, you can often sense Holy Spirit's leading as a gut feeling.

I had a feeling like this while driving home from work one day. I kept having a sense that I should go back to work. I knew Sally and the kids were waiting for me to have dinner, so I pushed the thought aside. But the closer I got to home, the more intense the feeling became. It became even stronger as I pulled into my driveway, so I decided to pull out and head back, even though I knew I'd have some explaining to do once I got home.

On my way back, I was stopped at a red light when I noticed a hubcap spinning in front of my car. For a split second I just watched it spin; then my brain kicked in: *Where did that come from?* Looking down the street, I could see that a sports car and an older car had collided just seconds before my arrival. I leaped from my car and raced to check on one of the drivers. Seeing she was okay, I rushed to the other car. The driver's head was tilted back, he wasn't breathing, his skin had a gray pallor, and he had no pulse. As a trained emergency rescue worker, I knew what to look for and had every indication that this man had died on impact. I blew one breath of air into him and said, "Live, in Jesus's name."

At that moment I felt a tap on my shoulder and turned to see two ambulance attendants behind me, ready with their equipment. I knew them well; in fact, I'd trained both of them. I stepped back and watched as they transferred him to a stretcher and placed him in the ambulance. They raced off toward the hospital where I worked, and I followed.

When I arrived at the emergency ward, I noticed they weren't doing CPR on the driver, which surprised me. I asked the attendants about how they had treated him in the ambulance. They seemed unfazed, as if this were just another routine call. He was still unconscious, but when they had checked his vitals on scene, he had a normal heart rhythm and was breathing. I knew this man had no carotid pulse when I had checked him just seconds before the ambulance arrived. Clearly, something miraculous had happened!

The man was later moved to another ward in the hospital. Though alive, he was unable to speak because the damage done by the impact was extensive. In the days that followed, I would visit his room whenever I could to talk to him. Mostly I talked about Jesus and the goodness of God. I wasn't sure he could understand me, so I asked him to blink once for no and twice for yes. He was hearing me and could respond in that way. When I asked him if he would like to give his life to Jesus, he blinked twice, and I was able to lead him in prayer. The next day I returned to visit with him again, but he was gone. He had passed away during the night.

I don't know why this man wasn't healed, but I do know that I will see him in heaven, because God cared enough for this man that he asked me to turn my car around just in time to prevent him from

How do you know that a gut feeling is a nudge from Holy Spirit?

breathing his last before having a chance to give his life to Jesus. Holy Spirit leads and guides us to reach the people he loves, and it's beautiful when we can be a part of it.

I'm sure you've had many experiences where Holy Spirit led you with a gut feeling. We all do, but the trouble is that many times we don't recognize when we are being led this way because it seems so normal and natural. As a result, we miss opportunities to reach people in our everyday lives. But being led by Holy Spirit isn't deep and difficult. It just comes down to being obedient to his inner nudging.

How do you know that a gut feeling is a nudge from Holy Spirit? Here's the ironclad test: you will have peace about it. If you feel peace about the direction you sense God leading, keep going. If you don't feel a sense of peace, something is not right.

It's exciting to begin to work with Holy Spirit! When you think you are hearing from him, check it out. If someone repeatedly comes to your mind, give that person a call. Don't be weird about it. Just say, "You've been on my mind today," and see what the response is. The person may be having a rough day or might encourage you.

Holy Spirit may not give you a revelation about someone every day, but just keep practicing. You'll learn to discern when you are hearing from him.

No Big Deal

If you sense that you are hearing from Holy Spirit, don't make a big deal out of it. Just follow the leading, and let the accuracy of what you experience speak for itself. If Holy Spirit is guiding you, he will lead you to truth.

A friend once introduced me to two brothers who ran a company that was expanding worldwide. One was the chief executive officer and the other was the chief operations officer. Both were new believers, so after sharing the vision of their company with me, they asked if I would pray with them over their endeavors. I was happy to, and as I prayed for wisdom and direction, I began to get this sense that something was wrong. I had a powerful impression that someone from within was doing things that could potentially bring the entire company down.

Taking a chance, I said, "As we were praying, I got this feeling—and I could be totally wrong—but I think someone in your company is threatening to take down the whole business if you don't deal with him. And I think you already know who it is."

Often when I share the piece of information Holy Spirit has given me, more detail comes, but in this case that was the only impression I received. It was enough. The men looked at each other and admitted they did know whom I was referring to. It was their brother-in-law, the chief financial officer. The leading was accurate (which became even more clear in the weeks and months that followed). I had communicated it in a way that I could have shrugged it off if they had denied any problem or said, "I don't know what you mean, but we'll keep an eye out for that." But as soon as the words left my lips, it was obvious that they were well aware of the person I was referring to.

When you sense a leading from Holy Spirit, simply share it in a natural way. If the leading isn't correct, no amount of spiritual talk will make it true. If it's accurate, the truth of the situation will be enough to convince anyone involved.

I've found that the more we try to work up something unusual, the less effective it is. Really, we just have to let Holy Spirit do what he wants to do in the situation. You can be powerfully led in a business setting without coming across as someone who can't be trusted to make wise decisions.

If you are in a meeting to discuss your company's strategy for the upcoming year and inside God is telling you that it is all wrong, you don't have to stand up and announce, "God told me this is a bad idea." If you do that and you're wrong—and everyone is wrong sometimes—you'll be labeled a religious nut or you'll make it seem as though God can't make up his mind.

Just communicate that you have a bad gut feeling about the plans. Businesspeople understand the gut. If they go ahead against your recommendation and the project fails miserably, the next time you say that you have a bad gut feeling, they'll listen! Later, when they start to notice that you seem to have a lot of accurate gut feelings, they'll ask what your secret is, and the door will be opened for you to share your story.

We also need to be careful not to lay claim on the specific ways Holy Spirit works through us, as though we had an exclusive right to those abilities. "I'm a prophet," one will say. "I'm an intercessor," says another. Meanwhile, we're all prophets, healers, intercessors, and prayer warriors because Holy Spirit lives in each of us, and he wants to touch people through us any way he can. As the apostle Paul reminded believers in Corinth, the important thing is not whom Holy Spirit works through but that people are saved. Paul drove this point home when he said, "So you should earnestly desire the most helpful gifts" (1 Corinthians 12:31, NLT).

When you want to help someone, the best way to work with Holy Spirit is whichever way meets the person's need at that moment. The best thing for a sick person is healing, for example, so identifying yourself as a prophet is limiting. Holy Spirit wants to use you to heal someone one minute and speak truth to someone the next, so stay open and he'll be free to do so.

JUST LISTEN

On another occasion I experienced this "gut feeling" leading while overseeing an accident scene. As I assessed the scene, I came to an injured man who was lying on his stomach. Our team had stabilized his neck and completed all the protocols necessary to roll him onto the stretcher, but for some reason my stomach knotted as I neared him.

I asked them to stop what they were doing and pulled on a pair of gloves. As I reached my hand under his abdomen, slowly moving from the upper to the lower, my hand sank into damaged tissue. Reaching my other hand around him, I held his abdomen in and gave the team the okay to roll him over. Only then could we see that his lower abdomen had been cut from one side to the other. Had I not paid attention to that leading, this man's bowels would have spilled onto the ground as he was rolled over. Holy Spirit had worked through me to save him from what might have been a fatal event.

Notice that no angel appeared, nor did I hear an audible voice. All I had was a feeling, which I correctly interpreted as Holy Spirit's leading. I believe this is how the apostles were led most often in the book of Acts. Once, when Paul was ready to move on to another city, he sensed that Holy Spirit didn't want him to go there. He picked another direction, but again he sensed it was wrong. This happened twice before he felt impressed to go to Europe (see Acts 16:6–10). Holy Spirit knew where Paul needed to go.

You can become adept at sensing when Holy Spirit is speaking to you. All it takes is a bit of practice. Holy Spirit is a person. You get to know him the same way you get to know anyone. Talk to him. Ask his opinion. Tell him how you feel. Ask for help. Then pause to listen so you can have a dialogue, not a monologue. He will communicate with you.

———

Some people believe Holy Spirit speaks only under the most tightly controlled conditions. They believe Holy Spirit's presence is so fragile and fleeting that if anybody coughs in church or if the music isn't exactly right, it will break the mood and drive him away. If that were the case, we could never hope for Holy Spirit to give us direction at an accident scene, or a family dinner table, or at school, or work, or anywhere else that real life takes place.

Thankfully, the idea that Holy Spirit's presence is fleeting is totally inaccurate. Jesus didn't function in a perfectly controlled church atmosphere. He even performed the miracle of healing a man's ear during the chaos of his arrest! The disciples didn't operate in perfectly controlled situations either, yet signs and wonders followed them wherever they went.

Holy Spirit wants to work with you in the context of your everyday life as well. As you begin to listen to him, pay attention to your gut, and test what you hear, you will grow in your ability to follow him. It can become a natural part of your everyday life to the point where you hardly think about it. As you stay tuned in to Holy Spirit and connect with the people he wants to touch in a contemporary way, you're going to do extraordinary things!

14 Taking Off Your Floaties

Being Spirit Contemporary isn't about holding massive retreats where thousands are healed and thousands more give their lives to Christ. Although we need men and women to rise up and do this sort of ministry as well, that's not what being Spirit Contemporary is about. Being Spirit Contemporary is being the soccer mom who wants to reach out to another mom who is going through a messy divorce. It's being the grandma who is desperate for a way to help her grandson who has stopped going to church and is getting into the wrong crowd at school. Being Spirit Contemporary is about you being you, listening to Holy Spirit, and reaching out in ways that are natural to you, right where you are. Spirit Contemporary is a *you* thing; it's God working in *you* and through *you*. And that's incredibly powerful to the people around you.

You can partner with Holy Spirit to see the miraculous happen in your everyday life. It isn't complicated, and you don't have to become someone you're not. Holy Spirit will work with your personality, just as you are, today and every day. All you have to do is be willing and available. In this chapter, you'll read a collection of inspiring true stories of the Spirit Contemporary life. As you read, think about how naturally and normally Holy Spirit could work through your life if you just pay a little more attention and are willing to do what he's prompting you to do.

DANCING OFF THE DEATH BED

At the request of one of his good friends, I visited a man who had been given about twenty-four hours to live. Doctors were unable to diagnose his illness, but his organs were shutting down. When we arrived at the hospital, we found this father of eight was so weak that he could speak only in a whisper.

This man was a Christian, and as I talked about healing, he nodded confidently and kept interjecting, almost as if he wanted to impress me with his knowledge or work up what he thought would be the right level of faith to see Holy Spirit work. At one point he started to pray fervently, but I sensed he was trying to force a miracle rather than accept the free gift that was available to him.

As I spoke about healing and God's grace, I encouraged him to relax and take it in. After a while, he seemed to let go, so I laid hands on him and quietly spoke life into his body. Then I stepped back.

He turned to his wife and said, "I feel good." Then, a little louder and stronger, he said, "I feel like sitting up."

"Do it!" his wife said excitedly.

He sat up haltingly and seemed a bit dizzy, but he managed to swing his legs over the side of the bed. "I feel good!" he said again, even stronger. "I feel like standing!" He reached out for the IV pole beside his bed, and his wife helped him to his feet.

As he stood to his feet and turned to the side, we couldn't help but notice that his hospital gown was wide open and he had nothing on underneath!

"I feel good!" he repeated again, even more excited.

"You look good!" his wife squealed.

"I feel like dancing!" he said.

"Well, do it!" she bubbled.

With the IV pole in hand, he started to shuffle his feet across the floor as he danced around the pole, giving us a full view of his backside each time he came around. He didn't care; he was completely healed!

DISINTEGRATING CYST

I knew a woman who had been diagnosed with an ovarian cyst the size of a grapefruit. Doctors had given her a surgery date, but she really didn't want to have surgery. She decided she would continue to pray for healing up to that date, but she would have the surgery if necessary. Tests showed that the cyst didn't shrink, so she went into surgery as scheduled. But when the doctors came out after surgery to talk to her husband, they seemed confused and hesitant.

They told him they had opened her up to remove the cyst, but when they proceeded to tie it off, the growth disintegrated before their eyes. That was how they put it. They were concerned because they had all agreed on the need for surgery and now had to explain why they had performed the operation but removed nothing!

I don't know why the cyst disappeared during surgery and not before, but a miracle took place in front of an entire surgical team. Miracles don't always occur in ways we expect them to. Sometimes they happen instantly. At other times miraculous events progress gradually or in stages.

FROM DEATH'S DOOR TO DINNER

I had been invited into the home of a woman who was very ill with cancer and had requested prayer. Since I didn't normally make home visits, I gave her a few audio messages on healing to listen to. Her condition deteriorated rapidly, however, and her husband called again to say I had better come quickly if I was going to come at all.

When I arrived at their home, her husband met me at the door and let me know in no uncertain terms that he didn't believe in healing. He led me to the bedroom where she was lying, and I was shocked at how incredibly thin she was. The cancer had spread to her throat, so whenever she tried to speak above a whisper, she started to cough and choke violently and was barely able to catch her breath. The cancer had also spread to her stomach, bowels, and femur, which meant she could no longer eat or drink anything and was unable to bear any weight on her fragile leg.

I asked if she had listened to the teaching I had sent her on healing, and she nodded, smiling. I shared a few more thoughts on healing, but before long she slipped into sleep. She was only strong enough to stay conscious for a few minutes at a time. I stuck around, waiting for her to wake up, but it was incredibly awkward because her husband wouldn't speak to me.

When I noticed her eyes were open again, I sat near her and shared a few other encouraging stories from God's Word for several minutes until she fell asleep again. After about an hour of her coming and going like this, I could see a flicker of hope in her eyes. When I asked if she was ready to pray, she agreed.

She was so weak she couldn't lift her hand off the bed, so I gently took her hand to pray. But as soon as I touched her, before I even uttered a word, she raised both hands in the air and started to thank Jesus in a loud voice.

Her husband's eyes were wide with amazement. He rushed over, shouting, "What happened? What happened?" As I tried to explain, the woman swung both feet over the side of the bed and sat up next to me. She was leaning forward over the edge of the bed, still thanking Jesus.

I turned to face her husband, who had sat down next to me on the bed, and explained that I had simply been teaching her God's Word on healing. We continued to talk about it for a minute before the husband jumped up, looking wildly around the room. His wife was no longer in bed! She had gotten up on her own, walked into the bathroom, and locked the door!

He began banging on the door, demanding to know what she was doing. She assured him she was only having a bowel movement, even though her bowels were supposed to be so cancer ridden they no longer functioned.

After a few minutes, she came out of the bathroom wearing a housecoat and slippers and shocked us by announcing she was going into the kitchen to make herself something to eat.

I cautioned her to try sipping some water or broth first because she hadn't eaten in weeks, but she wouldn't listen. While she went to the kitchen, her husband peppered me with questions. He wanted to know how this miracle had happened, what was going on, what I had done to her, and what was going to happen next. Meanwhile, his wife cooked herself some food and sat down to eat it, just as I'm sure she had done hundreds of times before. It all happened so naturally. You would have never guessed she had been close to breathing her last just a few moments before.

About an hour later, the woman was standing in the kitchen when her daughter walked into the house. She took one look at her mom standing in the kitchen, dropped the books she was holding, and started to scream. Mom and Dad both rushed over, and there were tears and hugging and a lot more questions. And when I called the woman a few weeks later, she was on her way to her daughter's figure-skating class.

Miracles still happen, though they aren't always done in a theatrical way, like you see on TV. I didn't put on a show, commanding the woman to get up out of that bed. I went there to pray with her for healing, but I didn't know what would happen. If she hadn't recovered, I would have tried to build rapport with her husband in an effort to influence him for Christ. I'm not worried about what happens or how it happens. I pray, believe, and encourage, and I don't worry about the result.

DEAD BODY TURNS PINK

Almost every day I pray that everyone I put my hands on would be touched by Holy Spirit. I believe in faith that something powerful will transfer to every person I touch. Shortly after I began praying this way, I had an incredible experience. During one of my shifts at the hospital, another team arrived with a patient they had been performing CPR on for more than forty minutes. They probably should have declared him dead at the scene; rigor mortis had set in, so he had likely been gone for over three hours. But because they had begun CPR, they were obligated to continue until they reached the hospital. When they arrived, I joined their seemingly futile effort to revive the man.

Doctors were ready to declare him dead. But as soon as my hands touched his chest to take over CPR, the heart monitors, which had been showing a flat line, instantly registered a normal sinus rhythm. The doctors jumped into action. One shouted, "Stop CPR!" As soon as my hands left the man's body, the monitors went straight to flat line again. "Start CPR!" the doctor yelled, and the monitors jumped back to a normal sinus rhythm.

This is very unusual because when someone is in cardiac arrest, an abnormal rhythm occurs, not an intermittent normal rhythm. This happened several times, and the doctors tried various treatments to get his heart beating on its own. I could tell they were anxious because of this. The start and stop of the patient's heart rhythm was being recorded, which could reflect badly on the doctors when their superiors reviewed the case.

Gradually, however, the man's skin tone went from bluish-black to a pink, healthy-looking color. Sadly, the man's heart never did begin to beat on its own, so he was eventually declared dead.

As I was washing my hands afterward, one of the doctors stared at me for quite a while. Finally he said, "Good CPR," before slowly walking off.

I don't know why Holy Spirit fully heals in some cases and not others, and I don't need to know. My role is to be open and available for God to use me as he chooses.

No More Wheels

Miracles don't always happen the way we expect them to. I had been invited to speak at a church in Quebec, and while teaching about how much God loves and cares for us, I decided to pray for healing. Many miracles took place then and there. However, I noticed a man with a gray beard sitting in a wheelchair off to my right. For some reason he caught my attention, and I felt compelled to teach about gradual healing. I explained that sometimes we are healed instantaneously, but at other times healing takes place over time.

About a month later, the producer at Miracle Channel, the Christian television station where I serve as CEO, received an e-mail saying that one of the men who attended the service in Quebec had been featured on the front page of a newspaper. The article explained that the man was now able to walk for the first time in twenty-three years, and a picture showed him standing beside his wheelchair, grinning from ear to ear.

We later learned the whole story. As I recall, an injury to his back had left him with some feeling in his lower body but only limited movement. At the church service, the man reported, something began to happen in his body. At home later that night, he told his wife about it. The next day he felt a bit strange. The following day, his wife got up in the morning and was shocked to find him standing at the mirror grooming himself. He had gotten up on his own, not realizing what he was doing. He simply started his morning routine without thinking, which he hadn't been able to do in twenty-three years. Shocked friends and neighbors called the local newspaper, which published the article and photo.

This miracle happened gradually, and I never even laid a hand on that man. All I did was teach him what God's Word says about healing and recovery.

On another occasion I prayed for a few people after a church service, including a woman who requested prayer for her ankle. She had broken her ankle in an accident, and surgeons had fused the bones to repair the damage. As a result, she was unable to bend her ankle and walked very stiffly, with a pronounced limp. When I prayed, nothing seemed to change, and I could tell she was disappointed. Others had received instantaneous miracles that day.

> This miracle happened gradually, and I never even laid a hand on that man.

I said, "Don't look at how God works in others. That'll only cause you to lose faith. When you go home today, just keep thanking God for healing. Keep praising him for what he's doing." She thanked me and turned to leave while I stayed to pray for others.

After a few minutes, I heard a scream from the back of the church, and the woman with the fused ankle came running back into the service. She showed me her ankle, which she could now rotate with ease. She said she had followed my advice and was thanking God for her healing as she left the church. When she stepped off the curb and onto the road, she heard a loud cracking noise. At that moment she regained full mobility in her ankle!

God doesn't do things the same way twice. We can't put him in a box. Some people regain their health when they forgive someone who has hurt them. Others walk out their healing bit by bit, using conventional medicine or alternative medicine. Still others receive a miracle in their bodies when they let go of anxiety and begin to trust God.

It's pointless to try to create a formula or a system for how, when, and where to pray for people. Holy Spirit will not be bound by rules. If he were, you would only have to listen to him once and you'd know exactly what to do in all situations. Instead, he works through us as we maintain complete dependence on him. This relationship is built on open communication, trust, and a willingness to step out and do what he leads you to do.

THE FORESIGHT YOU NEED

Reading about these accounts of healing, you might get the idea Holy Spirit works in you *only* to benefit others. While it's true he wants to work through you to impact the world, Holy Spirit will work in *your* life also. He also isn't limited to performing miracles when you are down and out. He can heal you from cancer, but he can also lead you into a better level of health even if you're already relatively healthy. He can provide the money to put food on the table when you have none, but he can also lead you from a place of financial stability to success. In fact, some of the most incredible miracles you will experience are ones where he leads you to avoid trouble. Here's an example.

One day as I drove on the highway, I had a strong compulsion to pull over. I was following a semitrailer, and not far behind me was a red sports car. After resisting the feeling for a minute, I pulled onto the shoulder for a few minutes, feeling silly and wondering why I was wasting my time on the side of the road.

When I got back on the highway and drove a short distance, the reason became clear. The semi I had been following, the red car, and two other vehicles were piled up in a terrible accident. Holy Spirit had led me to pull over so I would miss an accident that would otherwise have been almost impossible to avoid.

On another occasion, I was in a restaurant having dinner when I had a strong feeling I shouldn't leave the restaurant through the front door. The sense became stronger as time went on, and by the time I paid the bill I was looking for other options. I took this seriously because, believe it or not, my family and I have received several death threats over the years.

I caused a bit of a scene when I decided to leave through the kitchen, where I walked past chefs and waiters yelling at me because I wasn't supposed to be there. I made it out the back door and to my car without any trouble, but I was curious why

Holy Spirit had led me that way. As I drove around to the front of the restaurant, the reason became clear. Two men were lurking outside—one on either side of the front door. One man held a knife.

I hadn't heard an audible voice warning me that someone was outside the restaurant waiting to jump me. It was just a gut feeling, but it probably saved my life.

The benefits Holy Spirit brings into our lives can't be counted. He will empower you to resist temptation, to make right choices in difficult circumstances, and to persevere through trouble. He will lead you to understand the truth you read in the Bible, open your eyes to see who Jesus is, and help you to realize what his plans are for the world and for you. He also reveals the truth about us, about the trustworthiness of others, and about what we need to live abundant lives.

While Holy Spirit definitely does perform survival-type miracles in your life, one of the most important benefits of the Spirit Contemporary life is that he leads you into sound choices that will make those last-minute interventions unnecessary. It's great to be miraculously restored to financial stability after a bankruptcy, but it's much better to get supernatural nudges toward making sound decisions that make bankruptcy unnecessary. Holy Spirit has all the foresight you need to live wisely.

This Is for YOU

I could name hundreds of examples of everyday people who have witnessed healing, experienced supernatural protection, and so much more. Each Sunday at Springs Church, we read a list of miracles like these, stories that have been reported to us by regular people, just like you.

Don't make the mistake of thinking that you have to be a pastor in order to see Holy Spirit work through you. All too often we create a gap between the laity—regular, everyday believers—and professional clergy. You may sometimes hear that certain people are "anointed" for different purposes, such as pastor, evangelist, or miracle worker. As a result, people travel thousands of miles to seek out a healing evangelist, believing that no one else can help them.

While that sounds very spiritual, it's not biblically correct. In the Old Testament, God did anoint only certain people, making it possible for them to have Holy

Spirit's power on or with them for a short time or a limited purpose (see Exodus 35:30–33; Numbers 11:17, 25–29; 1 Samuel 10:6, 10). But things are different now. When you gave your life to Jesus, Holy Spirit entered into you. His power isn't on you; it's *in* you. You are a brand-new creation that is filled with his power and ability, whether you realize it or not.

Holy Spirit's power for healing is in every person who has given his or her life to Christ. All of us! Working with Holy Spirit is not a privilege reserved for pastors or those in some full-time ministry. Holy Spirit will work with *you*, through *you*, in ways that are natural to *you*, if you are open and available.

Holy Spirit is calling you to live this Spirit Contemporary life. He's calling you to rise up and move on with him. If you're comfortable with how you've always related to him, you may be tempted to just keep things the way they are, but he's calling you to go deeper.

> **Holy Spirit will work with *you*, through *you*, in ways that are natural to *you*, if you are open and available.**

He's calling you to walk in water, not just up to your ankles but up to your knees. Then, when that becomes comfortable, he will call you to walk up to your waist. If you keep responding, there will come a time when you know you're attempting more than what you can do on your own. You've waded in until you can't touch the bottom. As you're being moved to and fro by the currents, it's going to be exciting, but it also might feel a little scary at first. You might be tempted to go back to what's comfortable, but you need to be willing to let go of your floaties and swim!

Remember, you're not doing this Spirit Contemporary life on your own. Let Holy Spirit take the lead. Keep pursuing more of God and his Word and stepping out in faith, and you will see the miraculous happen in your everyday life!

Part 5

ALL CONTEMPORARY

15 A Beautiful Mind

As a young person I witnessed many miracles in church and in our family. I believed God could do amazing things—in fact, my dad had been healed of a serious case of rheumatic fever that almost killed him when he was a teenager. Yet something troubled me. Most of the miracles I had witnessed or heard about took place in church.

Those miracles also closely followed a set of rituals that were supposed to encourage Holy Spirit to act. Although my parents were definitely the exception, many of the Christians I knew seemed to have preconceived notions about how Holy Spirit would and wouldn't work. They also seemed to expect nonbelievers to come to the church for the help they so desperately needed, rather than taking the power and love of God into the world.

When I studied the life of Jesus, I realized that's not how he operated. Jesus did miracles out in the world—at funerals, in homes, and on the sides of mountains. When he touched someone's life, it didn't follow a strict protocol. Each case was unique. And all of this took place in the context of normal life. It was not sensationalized, like so much of what I saw in churches and on television. In other words, I saw a huge gap between the way Holy Spirit operated in the lives of Jesus and the apostles and the methods I saw employed by most of the Christians I knew.

In time I came to see the reason for that. When believers around the world began to rediscover Holy Spirit, which happened in North America around the beginning of the twentieth century, people developed ways of hearing from and working with him. Some of those practices now seem odd, but they were doing things the best way they knew how. In any case, what worked for them in dealing with Holy Spirit simply didn't work for later generations.

Today, we realize we can never reach people in their everyday lives at work, at school, or in their neighborhoods using some of the rituals and practices handed down to us. Those methods just don't make sense to the average person.

As an emergency responder, I felt this disconnect strongly. I needed to know how to hear from Holy Spirit when I was wading in ditches filled with water and blood looking for accident survivors. I had to be able to sense his direction and access his healing power in a way that wouldn't make me seem unfit for duty at the hospital. I couldn't pull people out of their wheelchairs or scream at evil spirits—not without getting fired! I was searching for a way to work with Holy Spirit that I could use in everyday life. Though I couldn't put words to it at the time, I was looking for a way to grow in favor with others, just as Jesus had done. In time, I realized that growing in favor involved putting others at ease. It's that simple.

How People Feel

I was on a flight to Australia one day when I struck up a conversation with the man sitting beside me. As we got to know each other, I found out that he was a successful businessman who ran multiple companies, and we really hit it off. We laughed, talked, and swapped ideas and stories about business, leadership, and management.

A couple hours into the flight, he shared with me that he was gay and detailed some of the persecution he had faced in the business world. Some of the things people had said and done to this man were appalling, and the worst of it all was that some of this persecution had come from his Christian friends. As he shared his heart, I just listened and agreed wholeheartedly with him about how ignorant and cruel people can be. Whether I agreed with his lifestyle choice or not wasn't relevant; I felt terrible for this man who had been treated so cruelly.

After a while, the subject came up of what I did for a living. As soon as I told him I was a pastor, his countenance changed. Not only did his facial expression change but he actually turned his entire body away from me in his seat.

"Now just a minute," I protested. "That's not fair. People judge me and treat me differently because of my beliefs, just like you. And I've done nothing but accept and support you this whole time, but now I'm feeling really judged by you."

"You're right," he said apologetically, turning to face me. For the rest of the long flight we got along famously. He listened to me share my point of view because I had listened to, honored, respected, and encouraged him as he shared his stories. And who knows? Maybe a few seeds were planted in his heart that day!

To gain favor with your neighbors, think about how your actions affect them.

Growing in favor with people really comes down to how you make people feel. It involves learning to fit into social situations. It's being excellent at what you do so your coworkers' jobs become easier. It also means having integrity.

To gain favor with your neighbors, think about how your actions affect them. If your house needs a paint job, your old vehicle is an eyesore in your driveway, and your barking dog keeps everyone up all night, how will your neighbors feel about you? Will they be open to your invitation to come to church, or will they be so annoyed with you that they won't listen to anything you have to say? You need favor with people—rapport, relationship, trust, admiration—to impact their lives. This is not to say that you have to be perfect to share your faith. If that were true, none of us could. But if you have no connection or influence with a person, why would that person want to hear what you have to say?

Gaining favor with others is important because people need to accept you and be willing to listen to you before you can influence their lives in any way. If they don't accept you, they won't benefit from what Holy Spirit has to offer through you—healing, encouragement, peace, a life-changing relationship with him—even if you're trying your best. Favor has to come first.

If you doubt this, remember that Jesus couldn't do many miracles in his hometown. When Jesus returned to the streets where he grew up, people couldn't wrap their heads around what he had come to do. Even though Jesus had done nothing to lose favor with those people, they didn't respect his spiritual authority simply because they were too familiar with him. *Who does Jesus think he is?* they wondered. *We've known him all his life. He's that carpenter's son, not a healer or teacher.*

Jesus recognized what was happening and said, "A prophet is not without honor except in his own town, among his relatives and in his own home" (Mark 6:4). Because Jesus had no favor with the people there, they couldn't receive anything from him. Verse 5 adds, "He could not do any miracles there, except lay his hands on a few sick people and heal them."

To influence people for Christ, you need to first gain their favor. Unfortunately, Christians often bulldoze ahead and share their faith before doing the work to gain favor. That always does more harm than good.

POWERFULLY ATTRACTIVE

A pastor once told me his church was small because Holy Spirit's presence was so strong there that people who had sin in their lives couldn't bear to stay around. Maybe that made the congregation feel better, but it sounds nothing like what we know of Jesus. People from all walks of life were drawn to him by the thousands. Jesus had the anointing of Holy Spirit without measure, yet sinful people flocked to him. That's because he was motivated by love for others and had deep compassion for what they experienced in life. That compassion motivated him to teach in a way they could understand.

When you are motivated by love, you communicate the message of Jesus in a way that fits the unique character and personality of the person you're speaking to. That may look different from person to person, even within the same family. When you are motivated by love, you don't care who gets credit for a person accepting Christ, and you don't rely on canned religious jargon. You put others first and take time to know them before trying to offer spiritual counsel.

Everyone longs to be understood. God has placed over seven billion beautiful minds on this planet, and when you take the time to understand people and communicate personally with the people you encounter, you will become powerfully attractive to them. As a result, Jesus will be attractive to them too.

If we could get beyond our prepackaged ways of thinking about the gospel and the people who need it and get back to the love Jesus had for people and his unique ways of relating to them, we would be amazed at the results. Continue to work with Holy Spirit, but approach each person and each situation in a way that gains favor before you try to respond. When you are guided by Holy Spirit *and* make it easy for people to accept what you have to say, there's no telling what might happen!

16 Green Apples

The most powerful way to grow in favor with others is to respect them.

Everyone longs to be respected. Don't you? When you feel the respect of others, it inspires you to do and be more. It makes you feel great. Respect is also attractive. You move toward those you respect. And if you communicate that respect to others, they also move toward you. Everyone loves a contagious smile and well-groomed appearance, but people are most powerfully drawn to those who make them feel good about themselves.

The reality is that until you respect others and win their respect, they will not open their hearts to what you have to say.

I don't think we as believers realize how arrogant we sound sometimes. We know we're right, and we profess to have all the answers because the Bible is our authority. But to those who don't yet trust what the Bible has to say, we come across as pushy and intolerant. It can seem to others that we are trying to show how smart we are and how stupid they are. If we never show respect for their point of view, our confidence comes across condescending, and it's a huge turnoff.

One of the best ways to communicate respect is to listen more than you talk. When you listen to people, it shows that you care about their lives and respect their opinions and beliefs. As they share their beliefs and their life stories, Holy Spirit will show you an open door to share your story. Your personal story of who Jesus is to you and what he's done in your life is infinitely more powerful than any argument could ever be.

To become Spirit Contemporary, you need to grow in favor with others. That means respecting them and gaining their respect in return, but you may need to overcome a few obstacles first.

RESPECT FIRST

One obstacle to building respect with others is we often disrespect them without realizing it. Taking a step back to see the interaction through the other person's perspective makes all the difference. For example, a number of Asian friends have shared with me how difficult it was for them to give their lives to Christ in their culture. Some were told by Christians that they had to renounce all ties to their family's religion, which sometimes included ancestral worship.

Although it is true you can't worship God and your ancestors at the same time, these sincere people were not given any help in making the transition away from their traditional religious practices. Instead, they were instructed to cut themselves off from all family gatherings related to this practice. By doing so they were disowned by their families because of the heartache and grief they caused.

I certainly don't suggest it's okay to worship your ancestors, but some of my friends have chosen to handle this problem in a more contemporary way. Instead of cutting themselves completely off from their families, and thereby cutting off any chance to influence them for Christ, they make every effort to honor their deceased loved ones—without worshiping them.

One man told me that when his father passed away, he performed the ceremonies required of him as the eldest son but changed the wording to communicate how much he respected and honored his dad, without crossing the line to worshiping him. This allowed him to maintain relationships with his family members and empowered him to reach them for Jesus!

Although there may be times when we need to stand for Christ even though it brings persecution, we don't have to go out of our way to alienate those who don't share our faith. It's almost as though some believers feel more spiritual when they are ridiculed. Often they have done little to prevent these negative reactions to their faith. In fact, the disrespect they show to others is often the cause of those reactions.

Because the Spirit Contemporary life is based on respecting others, it is the most effective method of bringing the gospel to other countries, other cultures, and people of other religions. It begins with recognizing the differences between Christianity and culture. In an effort to reach people for Jesus, many Christians have made terrible mistakes in this area over the years.

People don't have to adopt our culture to accept Jesus.

For example, the way missionaries reached the First Nations people in North America was inexcusable. These ill-informed missionaries believed that they had to rip these people from their culture in order to reach them. They forced European culture on them, as well as their own religious rules. The results have been devastating.

People don't have to adopt our culture to accept Jesus. Often we are unable to tell the difference between the two, and we lump our faith in Jesus, our culture, and even our political viewpoints into one package. By doing so, we turn many people away from the faith, and those we do influence are more likely to be converted to our culture than they are to be inspired to develop a relationship with God through Christ. But if we work with Holy Spirit, he'll show us how to bring Jesus to the people of any culture in a way that's contemporary to them.

For example, what would you say to a man from another culture who gives his life to Christ but has four wives and has fathered children with each one? Before he gave his life to Christ, his having more than one wife may have been completely acceptable in his society. Now what? Should he pick one family to keep and kick the rest out? What if a person who has undergone surgical treatment for a sex change comes to Jesus? Would we tell that person to get it reversed? These are tough questions, and I don't pretend to have all the answers. But I do know that anyone who loves Jesus is on the right track, and we need to all grow and learn together. We begin by respecting people as they are, where they are. No real Spirit work is possible without that foundation.

There are times when it is necessary to draw a firm line, but we have to resist inflicting judgment on others. Teach them about Jesus; then back away to let Holy Spirit work.

Don't Pick the Green Ones

I used to love debating with people about my faith. I was always ready with an answer in case someone asked me a question, and I usually did well at proving my case. I noticed though, over the years, that those arguments rarely or never resulted in people giving their lives to Christ. Arguing about spiritual topics is more about our pride than a sincere desire to reach people for Christ. And people who want to debate with you about your faith are usually just looking for a sparring partner; they're not ready to start a relationship with Jesus. So I stopped debating with people. Instead, I now communicate that I accept each of them as a person and reach out a hand in friendship. I can't force them to believe what I believe—and I don't want to force them—but we can still be friends.

I call these people green apples, because they're not ready to receive Jesus. Have you ever tried to pick a green apple? As you yank on it, the whole branch bends under the pressure. If you're not careful, you'll break off the entire branch. You could damage the fruit just by pulling so hard. It's easy to do that with people. When they're not ready to give their lives to Jesus, pressuring them will do no good—and may result in harm.

Often we feel as if we have to "close the deal" when sharing our faith with others. We have a sense of urgency about eternity, and we want them to be saved *now* because tomorrow could be too late. We feel as if we should do anything and everything to get them to invite Jesus into their lives right this very minute. While it's good to have a sense of urgency about sharing our faith, remember how Paul characterized the process of evangelism. He compared it to a garden. Some plant the seeds, others water, and still others reap the harvest (see 1 Corinthians 3:6).

Evangelism is not a solo competition. In fact, it's not a competition at all. It's a team effort, and it often takes time. When we get to heaven we'll see that those we have led to Jesus have actually been reached through the efforts of many people over time. When you are in touch with Holy Spirit and attentive to those around you, you will find many opportunities to play a role in the salvation of others.

Jesus said the fields are ready for harvest (see John 4:35). There are a whole lot of red apples out there, ripe for the picking. Because their hearts have been prepared in advance by Holy Spirit and the combined efforts of many others, all you have to do is gently nudge them toward Jesus. Others are still green, not ready for harvest. Respect that. Respect them. Your interactions with them, even if Jesus never comes up, may be a part of their preparation to one day make the decision to follow Christ.

17 LAF Culture

The world is filled with imperfect people. We are all flawed. We make mistakes, and we hurt one another—sometimes intentionally, often unintentionally. Getting along with others is a messy business. That makes it crucial that we embody grace. To gain favor with others, we have to treat them with the same dignity and openness that Jesus displayed.

There are three characteristics we all need to embody in our relationships with others, and these three make all the difference. When you keep growing in these qualities, you're sure to grow in favor with others, which opens the door for you to influence them for Christ. It's easy to remember these key characteristics of the Spirit Contemporary life with a simple acronym: LAF. I like to pronounce it "laugh" as a reminder that it's okay to enjoy life, and it stands for *love, accept,* and *forgive.* To grow in favor with others, you have to LAF more.

When you love, accept, and forgive others, you enjoy relationships on an entirely new level. LAF both improves how you feel about relationships with others and also makes them want to be around you. Think about it: Would you rather be around people who love and accept you and are quick to forgive you when you fail? Or would you rather be around people who judge you, are easily offended, and hold grudges? It's not a hard decision. No one enjoys being judged and shamed; everyone responds to grace.

Determining to LAF more is a personal decision, but it's more than that. Years ago, Sally and I made the decision to build a life-giving church. We wanted a church where people knew they were loved, accepted, and forgiven. Every group—every business, church, family, or team—has a culture. Some group cultures attract people; others repel them. Some businesses seem to draw great employees; others can't hold on to good help. Some brands create such a great atmosphere that their customers can't stop talking about them. With others, customers can't stop talking either, but it's all negative.

Sally and I realized that culture is always created, but it isn't always intentional. If you don't take the time to think through the culture you're creating in your church, family, or team, it will still have a culture—but it may not be the one you would choose. As the architects of the culture in our church and our family, we chose to create a LAF culture. And while we're not perfect, we aim to LAF every day.

The culture you create in your church, your family, your community, or wherever you are can help you grow in favor with others and win them to Christ, or it can stand in your way. Culture is foundational because it affects every interaction you have with others. The culture you promote (or tolerate) communicates to others what is acceptable and unacceptable in the group. So when parents allow their kids to speak disrespectfully of others or spread gossip, they create a culture of disrespect in their home. They silently communicate that it's okay to be judgmental. When you are quick to forgive others, you create a culture of love and acceptance.

It's vital that you set the culture in your interactions with others. To be Spirit Contemporary and really connect with people, they need to feel that they are entering a place of love, acceptance, and forgiveness when they're around you.

LOVE

When we talk about loving others, we're not talking about mushy, romantic love. To love people the way Jesus loved is to demonstrate that you value them.

Every person on this planet wants to feel valuable. They want to know that they matter to someone and that their lives count for something. God loves each and every person this way, not just those who believe in Jesus. John 3:16 says, "For God so loved the world that he gave his one and only Son, that whoever believes in him shall not perish but have eternal life." God loved us *before* we believed in Jesus, and he loves people this way still. And he's counting on us to show people this love.

Showing people that you value them is one of the greatest gifts you can give, and it transforms your relationships with them. When people know they are valued, they are set free to grow and become all that God has created them to be. Pointing fingers at people for their problems or failures does nothing good, especially with people who don't know Jesus. That only drives them away from the solution they desperately need—Jesus. We need to begin by loving others, valuing them as the magnificent creations of God that they are, and set the foundation for them to enter into the one relationship that has the power to transform everything in their lives.

A popular saying holds that "people don't care how much you know until they know how much you care." That sums it up exactly. When people know they are loved unconditionally, they feel the freedom to change and grow. Love first. That works in families, and it works in churches. People respond to love.

How can you love people this way? Keep your heart humble and full of God's love, and his love will flow from you to those who need him. They will sense this love, and it will make you powerfully attractive to others. And when you're motivated by love, you'll place your personal preferences second. If you like to speak a certain way but it makes someone else uncomfortable, you adapt. If you like old gospel hymns at church but you know that a newer style will reach more people, you learn to love the new.

People realize when they are being manipulated, and they realize when others are willing to sacrifice for them. Love is a powerful force.

ACCEPT

To love others is to value them. And when you value others you accept them as they are. Most people are conscious of their mistakes and realize that they aren't perfect. When you accept others without judgment, you become a safe person to be around.

That gains tremendous favor, which opens the door to bring good news into their lives.

Where there is no acceptance, people suffer. When family members judge one another rather than accept one another, marriages can't thrive and children look for the first opportunity to leave home. Acceptance, and the safety it brings, is the foundation for healthy family relationships. It allows people to tolerate one another's shortcomings more patiently and enjoy all the differences.

A church that lacks a culture of acceptance becomes judgmental. But when a church demonstrates acceptance, people sense that they can belong, just as they are, and that is powerfully attractive.

It's not uncommon for people in our church to respond with an "Amen" or a "Yeah" when they hear a point they strongly agree with during a message. But one Sunday, while I was sharing a message about the culture of love, acceptance, and forgiveness we aim to create at our church, I heard something quite different.

I had just delivered a point when this sound came echoing up from the back row, overpowering all the Amen-ers in volume, but mostly in shock value. About fourteen rows back sat a man I had never seen before. I later found out that he had never been to church before, so when he heard other people expressing their agreement with "Amen," he responded in the best way he knew how to express strong emotion, with a "F——yeah!"

The first time he said it, there were a few shocked looks and muffled snickers that rippled through the audience. But the beautiful thing about this story is that even though he said the f-word *seven more times* throughout my message, no church members turned around to stare him down or shake a shaming finger at him. No ushers escorted him out. That man was accepted as he was, and at the end of the service, he gave his life to Christ.

> **God accepts all of us as we are, though he doesn't expect us to stay that way.**

In a culture of acceptance, you can still confront problems when necessary. The difference is you let Holy Spirit do the primary work on people's hearts. You see, God accepts all of us as we are, though he doesn't expect us to stay that way. He loves us too much to leave us in our current condition. He wants to help us grow and learn to become more like him. So, a culture of acceptance doesn't mean that we don't expect anyone to change and grow. It just means *we* stop trying to change them.

Now, when you ask Christians if they accept others, most would say, "Of course!" However, people's intentions and actions often don't line up. Some boast of having a church that accepts people from all walks of life, but in reality they merely tolerate them. There's a big difference between acceptance and tolerance. For example, a group of Christian guys in a workplace might say they accept their gay coworker yet never include him in conversations. That's not acceptance. We may be blind to that distinction, but others are not. People know when they are genuinely loved and wanted versus when their presence is merely tolerated.

To be clear, accepting others does not mean agreeing with everything they do. Acceptance is not an endorsement of behavior. It's desiring relationships with people regardless of the personal differences between you. It's respecting where they are on their journeys. It's valuing them as they are and not communicating that they have to change in order to be around you.

Acceptance is not blind trust either. It's not about allowing others to hurt you. You need to set healthy boundaries and require people to earn your trust. Acceptance is simply making a conscious decision to love others just as they are, while leaving it to Holy Spirit to change their hearts and lives.

Acceptance is one of the most powerful aspects of the Spirit Contemporary life because it allows people to belong to a loving community, just as they are. And everyone craves belonging.

FORGIVE

Love and acceptance lead naturally to forgiveness. When people know they are valued and feel certain they have a safe place to belong, they have the freedom to admit their faults and failures, knowing they'll be forgiven. Without forgiveness, we create a culture of pretending, because we're all imperfect. When we have to hide these imperfections, we lose authenticity. Nothing is more offensive to the world outside the church than phoniness or hypocrisy. Yet when we give people the freedom to fall and pick themselves up again without judgment, we point the way to Jesus.

It is impossible to respect people without a willingness also to forgive them. We all fail, and we all need forgiveness. And we all have many opportunities to forgive. When we realize how greatly we have been forgiven by God, it's impossible to withhold that forgiveness from others. Experiencing grace empowers you to give grace.

Each of us is hurt by others from time to time. When we forgive, we restore rather than destroy the relationships. Forgiveness is powerful, both for the one forgiven and for the one who forgives. In fact, healthy relationships can't develop without forgiveness because love and forgiveness are twins. You can't love if you will not forgive.

How do we forgive big offenses? We choose to. Forgiveness is not a feeling; it's a choice. Every time resentment and anger return, we can choose to respond with forgiveness. God has asked us to forgive, and he will also empower us to do it in Jesus's name. It may take time, but forgiveness is possible. And when we forgive, we open one of the most powerful doors to speaking into another person's life.

Forgiveness is the essence of the Spirit Contemporary life because it depends on having received grace (favor) from God and on giving grace (favor) to others. And it's the most freeing way to live!

LAF More!

The LAF concept may be easy to understand, but it isn't always easy to apply. How do you accept people whose lifestyles are so different from your own? How do you love those who seem unlovable? Here are some simple steps to creating a LAF culture.

Find Common Ground

One day I was talking with a prominent member of Canada's First Nations people. As the conversation progressed, he shared some of his beliefs. For example, he believed that his drum had a spirit that would bring peace into the community where he played it. He also believed that when he gathered with a group to make decisions and they blew smoke from his pipe in all four directions, the spirit of his pipe would help them make wise decisions.

As I listened, I asked questions and was genuinely interested in what he believed. I was also looking for common ground, trying to figure out how to transition from what he believed to a conversation about my belief in Jesus. I began with this statement: "I can tell that you rely on the spirit realm a lot."

He agreed wholeheartedly. Then we talked about my reliance on the one we call Holy Spirit. I said that he reveals things to me, guides and leads me, heals people, and gives me information I could never know on my own. He was fascinated, and before we ended the conversation, he said he wanted to hear more about this Jesus who controls the spirit realm.

I didn't have to correct this man or talk down to him in order to share what I know of Holy Spirit. I simply piqued his interest, which led to future conversations about Jesus. You can find common ground with almost anyone, and by building on that commonality you open the door to sharing your faith.

Put Others on Equal Ground

When sharing the good news with others, many Christians feel they have to confront sin at every opportunity. Otherwise, they believe they are compromising their own faith. As a result, they heap guilt and shame on the very people they are trying to reach. That's not at all what Jesus did.

In Luke 19:1–10 we read that Jesus passed by a man named Zacchaeus, who had climbed a sycamore tree to get a better vantage point. Jesus looked up at Zacchaeus and called him by name, saying, "Come down immediately. I must stay at your house today" (verse 5).

Zacchaeus was the most unlikely person in the crowd to host Jesus for lunch. Zacchaeus was a tax collector, and it was common knowledge that tax collectors overcollected taxes from hard-working people and pocketed the difference. People hated tax collectors! So when Jesus announced he would be the guest of this "sinner," a murmur went through the crowd. How could a righteous person do such a thing? Remember, too, that sharing a meal with someone was a sign of friendship and acceptance in that culture. So with one statement, "I must stay at your house today," Jesus demonstrated unconditional acceptance of Zacchaeus. He lifted Zacchaeus from his shame-filled status and placed him on equal ground with everyone else.

Jesus didn't shame Zacchaeus for his wrongdoing. He didn't even mention it. Yet after having lunch with Jesus, Zacchaeus committed to giving half of his wealth to the poor and repaying fourfold anyone he had cheated (see verse 8). That's the power of grace.

On another occasion, religious leaders brought before Jesus a woman who had been caught committing adultery. She felt the sting of the crowd's judgmental, condemning looks as she stood helpless before them. But Jesus didn't look at her that way. When asked for his judgment on the matter, Jesus said, "Let any one of you who is without sin be the first to throw a stone at her" (John 8:7). Religious people had placed her in a gutter of shame, but Jesus placed her on equal ground with every self-righteous person there. Although he didn't excuse her behavior, Jesus accepted her as a person. She didn't need to earn his love, acceptance, or forgiveness. Jesus showed her grace.

Without love and acceptance, there can be no trust and no possibility of relationship. The reality is, people need a safe place of love, acceptance, and forgiveness in order to respond to Holy Spirit. When we place people on equal ground, showing that we love and accept them just as they are, we create an environment where change is possible.

Don't Judge

When we refuse to accept people the way they are, we become judgmental. We assume we know why people do what they do, but only God can know a person's heart (see 1 Kings 8:39). We simply don't have the ability to judge others, and when we try to, we bring pain and limitations to that relationship. Here's an example.

Let's say a mom is hosting a birthday party for one of her adult sons. This mom always hosts the best birthday parties for her kids, and she invites the whole family over to celebrate. However, on this particular birthday, the son can't help but notice that the party seems less impressive than those she'd given before. She usually baked a chocolate cake, his favorite, but this time all she has is a stale, store-bought white cake. She gave each of his siblings a wonderful gift for their birthdays, but it's clear she didn't put much thought into what she bought for him. Something isn't quite right.

This son has a choice to make. He could ask, "Mom, what happened? Is everything okay?" She might explain that she had a terrible week, filled with one disaster after another, and had simply run out of time to plan his party. In that case, he would sympathize with the pressure she was under, and it would be a finished issue. Even if he was a little disappointed, he would quickly let it go.

Or he could choose to judge his mom without opening up a conversation. He could allow himself to think, *My siblings got their favorite cakes, great gifts, and fun parties. But I get dried-out cake, a lousy gift, and a boring party. I can put two and two together. Mom just doesn't love me.* By doing so, he would be judging her motives and her intentions, not merely assessing her behavior, and that always brings trouble to a relationship. Judgment opens the door to pain and resentment.

I have counseled many people who have destroyed a lifetime of beautiful relationships by judging the hearts of others. Meanwhile, learning to LAF more means suspending judgment, opening conversations, and building relationships. It causes you to grow in favor with others, which is such a key component to living the Spirit Contemporary life.

Live and LAF

Jesus demonstrated this culture of loving, accepting, and forgiving throughout his life. The LAF culture may be challenging to create, but it's worth fighting for. It's also a crucial aspect to becoming Spirit Contemporary.

The culture you create in your church, your home, and your personal life gives people a framework to understand how people will be treated in those contexts. Those cultures determine what happens when people make mistakes—whether they will be shamed and ridiculed or accepted and coached. A culture that lacks love, acceptance, and forgiveness is crippling, but when people sense they can risk failure rather than being rejected for their mistakes, they will feel safe and begin to grow.

Create an atmosphere around you where people can love, laugh, and enjoy one another—imperfections and all—and you will have an incredibly attractive culture everywhere you go. You won't believe how powerfully God can work in an environment like this!

18 The Power of Your Story

Have you ever noticed that most of the accounts of Jesus's work on earth involve one-on-one interactions? Only a few of Jesus's public messages are recorded in the Bible. The rest of what we know about him comes through conversations with individuals—a widowed woman, a blind man, a Samaritan woman. Jesus often reached one person at a time.

It's tempting to believe that only pastors who speak to thousands can make a difference, but if we are to impact our cities, our nations, and our world, we need to get back to this basic principle: God changes the world one person at a time.

That makes your personal story of how Jesus has made a difference in your life the most powerful tool you have for reaching others with the gospel. When someone is open to hearing it, you can share the story of your life—the pain, heartaches, victories, and losses. As you share your experience of finding answers, hope, and even miracles when you found Christ, you reach straight to the heart of another person. No one will argue with your personal experience if you keep it real, don't exaggerate, and are not arrogant, condescending, or pushy. Rather than debating others, which only pits your beliefs against theirs, just share what happened to you. Personal stories are always interesting, and there's great power in sharing what Jesus has done for you.

When sharing our faith with others, we sometimes feel that we need to have all the answers. We feel pressed to debate evolution, defend certain doctrines, or prove that the Bible is really true. When we deal with others who are going through a tough time, we think we need to provide the perfect solution to every problem or explain why bad things happen. All of that serves to alienate people who don't agree. It's pointless. Instead, the most effective thing you can do is talk about what you've witnessed. Talk about the subject you are the expert on: what Jesus has done in *your* life.

NO COINCIDENCE

Many people feel hesitant about sharing their stories because they're not sure others would care, or they're not sure what to say. As with all aspects of the Spirit Contemporary life, this actually comes quite naturally.

Remember Paul's teaching in 1 Corinthians 3:6: "I planted the seed, Apollos watered it, but God has been making it grow." That's a reminder that any good results that come from our efforts are really God's doing. He makes it happen; we just play whatever small role is assigned to us. It doesn't have to be complicated. I just try to keep my eyes open for opportunities to share what I know of Jesus. Sometimes I notice a particular person in a store or restaurant, and I pray, *Okay, Holy Spirit, what's your plan here? If you want me to share my story with this person, direct the way.* Sometimes I pray silently for the person and move on, but if I sense Spirit's leading, I look for a way to strike up a conversation.

That doesn't always lead to something, but sometimes it results in a conversation about Jesus, church, or some aspect of faith. I don't feel the need to "close the deal" by praying a prayer of salvation with each person. I realize I may be just planting a seed that will take root later. I have heard from people, years afterward, that they started going to church because of a few words we exchanged in a store, words that came to their minds when the time was right.

On one occasion I was in a department store to buy a pair of gloves when I noticed an older gentleman also looking at the glove display. I had a sense I should talk to him, so I struck up a conversation by asking if he had seen any extra-large gloves.

He nodded and handed me a pair. As I was trying them on, I asked, "How are you doing today?"

"Ah, not very good," he said.

We opened a conversation in which he shared that his wife was dying, and I listened as he related his heart-wrenching struggle. I didn't do anything extraordinary. I genuinely wanted to hear his story. I listened, and he seemed very grateful. As a result, I was able to mention the church I serve and invite him to come. I didn't feel the need to say more. I simply planted a seed.

If I had felt Holy Spirit guiding me to lead the man to pray and invite Jesus into his life, I would have done so. But I sensed this man wasn't yet ready. However, he was deeply moved that I had taken time out of my own day to brighten his, and he thanked me profusely. I had the feeling this conversation would not be soon forgotten.

One person coming to Christ usually involves several interactions leading up to that decision. A believer shares a kind word or a bit of encouragement with someone, and the person is deeply touched. Later, when another Christian does something kind for that person, prays with her, or invites her to church, she is more open because of the first interaction. In time, yet another believer has the privilege of leading that person to accept Jesus. Each one plays a small part; one isn't more important than another.

Don't worry about when to approach a person or what you will say. When you hear from Holy Spirit, your timing and words will be just right. In the case of the man in the department store, the "coincidence" of someone listening sympathetically on a particularly low day spoke much louder than if I had tried to share a message with him. Just follow Holy Spirit's lead, speak in a natural, ordinary way, and leave the results to God. When you do, you'll be involved in "coincidental" meetings all the time.

YOU GOTTA SEE THIS MOVIE!

Sharing your story in a Spirit Contemporary way comes quite naturally. You probably use this method all the time without realizing it when you share new experiences with people so they can benefit from them. When you enjoy a movie, you tell all your friends to see it too. If a car salesman gets you a great deal, you tell everyone you know to use that dealership. When you see results from a diet or exercise plan, you share it with your friends. Influencing others in this way is a natural thing to do, and it's usually much appreciated.

When you tell a friend about a new restaurant, do you feel the need to explain every detail about the menu? Probably not. You don't need to have all the answers. You just passionately communicate what you do know, and your friend senses the enthusiasm. Sharing your story about Jesus is much like that. No one expects you to know everything about the Bible or complicated theological issues. They want to hear your heart, your passion, what you've experienced. That's what will influence them.

Many Christians think they have to debate with others and prove the validity of their beliefs. They hesitate to share their faith because they're afraid they don't have all the answers. In fact, logical arguments rarely bring people to Christ. Logic alone can't convince individuals that God loves them or wants to heal them or help them in some way. Only Holy Spirit's power flowing through you can blast through the objections and touch people's hearts to produce real change. Besides, sharing your story isn't about you. You're connecting with others so Holy Spirit can do his work.

Remember, Jesus didn't call all of us to be theologians or apologists, able to formally defend our beliefs through reason. He called each of us to be *"witnesses"* (Acts 1:8), and a witness is simply someone who has seen or experienced something and can testify to it. If you are asked to be a witness in court about a car accident, it is because you saw, heard, or experienced something to do with that accident. The court is looking for your firsthand account of what happened, not expert testimony on traffic laws. A witness is someone with an experience to share. That's it. So when you share your story, that's all you're doing—telling what you have experienced when it comes to Jesus.

Your experience doesn't have to be sensational to be powerful.

Your experience doesn't have to be sensational to be powerful. When I was a young person, our church often invited guest speakers to share their testimony with the youth. These guests always seemed to have jaw-dropping, turnaround stories. Often they told of having been drug dealers, or of being wildly promiscuous, or drinking heavily. We would stare wide-eyed as these speakers wowed us with their former lifestyles and then, in the last two minutes, told of giving their lives to Christ and giving up the life of sin. We were left to assume that only those with a sensational testimony could bring others to Christ. It seemed as though we needed to go out and sin a bit just so we would have compelling stories!

I thank God I never went in that direction, but because I'd been so conditioned to believe that personal testimonies had to be juicy to be effective, I thought I had nothing to share with others. At the age of eighteen, I was invited to share my testimony with a group, and I was sure I had nothing to say. Since I had already agreed to speak, I had to think of something, and after giving it some thought and prayer, I realized I was a witness after all. I hadn't experienced a crazy life, but I had experienced Jesus's saving and keeping power. He had protected me from drug abuse, violence, and many other terrible things, and I could share that.

Your testimony doesn't have to sound like anyone else's. In fact, it shouldn't. It's *your* story. Just tell what Jesus has done for you.

LET 'EM HAVE IT . . . PASSION, THAT IS

In conversation with a young man one day, he realized I was a pastor and went on a rant about what he believed. He didn't hold back and wasn't very polite. In situations like this, many Christians get sheepish and respond with "It's good to have strong beliefs" or something equally weak, then change the subject. I took a different approach.

I let him speak his mind, and I listened intently. I was very respectful. But when he was finished, I asked if I could tell him what I believed. Because I had taken the time to listen to him respectfully, he was open to what I had to say. I told him about the power of Jesus I've experienced in my life. I spoke politely, but with even more passion and confidence than he had displayed. He seemed surprised, possibly because had never met a Spirit Contemporary Christian before.

You see, when other people speak with confidence, their confidence is based on themselves. But when a Spirit Contemporary Christian speaks with confidence, the power of Holy Spirit flows through every word, and that power impacts people at their deepest level. As I shared about my relationship with Jesus and how he has made me stronger than I've ever been, something touched this man's heart—and it wasn't me. Tears began to flow down his cheeks, and he gave his life to Jesus that day. That didn't happen because my experience is better than anyone else's or because I know the Bible so well. It happened because I was willing to share with passion about the power of God in my life, and you can do that just as easily.

Your story might be that you began to sleep better and feel more at peace when you started coming to church, or that your relationship with your spouse is closer than ever, or that you get angry with your kids less often. Maybe you're not exactly sure when that happened. There's no need to manufacture details or exaggerate to make your story sound more impressive. When you fake it, people can tell. Your actual experience is a great testimony, and it's all you need.

Some people hesitate to share what God has done for them because their biggest moments occurred many years ago. But your story is still just as powerful today as it was then. The most recent miracle in the Bible happened two thousand years ago, yet it still builds people's faith!

> **Telling people about Jesus and helping them decide to follow him will be the greatest adventure of your life.**

Share your story with passion. In fact, I want you to write down your story. Make a list of the things God has done in your life: loving you, forgiving you, giving you freedom, providing miracles and protection, leading you, encouraging you. Review the list to keep it fresh in your mind. Then share your stories.

Telling people about Jesus and helping them decide to follow him will be the greatest adventure of your life, and the most effective way to do it is to share your story with people in everyday life. When you do that the same way you would talk about a great movie or a restaurant you enjoyed, it will be easy and people will want to listen. Just be yourself. Let Holy Spirit do the rest.

Part 6

RISK IT AND LIVE IT

19 Taking Risks

Christians often focus their outreach efforts on people who are obviously hurting—the poor, sick, dying, depressed, and those in crisis—but they aren't the only ones who need Jesus. Every person who doesn't know Jesus is facing a huge crisis. There's no bigger problem people can have than to face eternity without Christ, and we never know when that moment will arrive.

When our children were young, we had a neighbor who came over to visit with Sally nearly every day. This lady's kids were a little out of control, and those visits took a toll on Sally. One day she said to me, "I want to help her, but I can't do this anymore." I knew how draining those visits were, so we agreed to pray that either our neighbor would change or we could find a polite way to have her over less often.

The next day, the woman came to our house as usual and during her visit told Sally that she couldn't wait to come over each day. She related that her home seemed so sad but ours was happy. There was laughter and fun, and she was amazed at how our kids listened to us. This neighbor could also sense the love Sally and I share, and she wanted that in her marriage.

That was an open door for Sally to share why our home was different. She talked about her relationship with Jesus and the difference it had made in her life. The next

Sunday we brought our neighbor and her kids to church with us. She gave her life to Christ in that service and kept coming week after week, even though her husband showed no interest.

One day we invited the whole family over for a barbeque, and as I was flipping burgers on the grill, I had a few minutes to talk with her husband. He confided that he had noticed a change in his wife. He could see she was treating him better, and he noticed his kids had changed as well. They were listening to their parents more, and their home seemed happier. Finally he asked, "Are they putting all this on just to get me to church?"

I laughed and shook my head, explaining this wasn't an act. It was an actual change in their lives. We talked about the emptiness he felt and the fact that it couldn't be filled with anything but Jesus. Then I invited him to church. He came the next Sunday, and he gave his life to Christ as well. I was thrilled at this change in his life and in their family, and I thought that was the end of the story—but there was more to come.

About six months later, the woman was diagnosed with stomach cancer. She fought the disease for four months before that fateful day when her husband and children had to say good-bye or, more accurately, "See you later in heaven." Her husband maintained his relationship with Christ after her passing, and I couldn't help but wonder what would have happened to this awesome couple if they hadn't discovered a relationship with Jesus.

It also made me think about the other families around every one of us that are struggling while we are unaware. Down your street, a little boy knows that when Daddy wakes up, he will give his son a beating. A woman who dreamed of being a princess when she was a little girl has just had another child, even though she feels trapped in a loveless marriage. A man is married to a woman who constantly attacks his self-worth to the point that he is discouraged enough to consider suicide. Meanwhile, we go about our lives each week, choosing not to see the needs of people around us.

Living the Spirit Contemporary life involves reaching out to the people around you. That can be intimidating because it involves taking the first step and revealing something about yourself, but it's always worth the risk. After all, your willingness to let Holy Spirit work through you will make an *eternal* difference in the lives of the people right around you.

LOOK AROUND

In Mark 16:20 we read that as the disciples stepped out into the world, "the Lord worked with them and confirmed his word by the signs that accompanied it." As you step out of your comfort zone to engage others, remember that Holy Spirit is always with you. It's not complicated or difficult. You just have to be available.

Let me give you an example. I was a regular at a coffee shop where I often saw another customer who frequented the place. He was lean and muscular, likely a bodybuilder, and he seemed to stare at me every time I saw him. It was unnerving. One day he approached my table and just stood there with his arms crossed, looking down at me. "I'm stronger than you," he finally said.

"Absolutely," I replied, "I can see that."

He said it again: "I'm stronger than you," and I was a little concerned about where this was heading. Fortunately he added, "But you have more power than me. Talk to me."

I invited him to take a seat across from me. I didn't have an eloquent speech prepared for that moment. I was just there and I was available. I explained that the power he sensed came from Jesus within me; it wasn't my own strength. I didn't get into any complicated doctrine. I just engaged him in respectful conversation and remained open to hearing from Holy Spirit. I led him to the topic of Jesus by talking about my story—what I know of Jesus. The conversation was unforced and natural because I didn't have an agenda. What I did have was genuine concern for this man and his spiritual journey. As I explained what Jesus had done for me, he told me that he wanted that too. He gave his life to Jesus that day.

Simply being available can open the door. But if we are never alert to the people around us, if we believe they don't want to hear about Jesus, or if we make ourselves too busy to get involved, nothing will happen.

CHOOSE CONFIDENCE

I often feel inadequate for the work Holy Spirit leads me to, but at a certain point in my life I made the decision to place my confidence in Jesus, not myself. If I didn't believe God would take my best efforts and work through them, I would quit my job today! Instead, I work hard and trust him to make it effective.

Despite what you feel are your limited abilities, God will honor your unwavering faith. You can make the decision to have confidence in Jesus and stand strong for him. That confidence will be attractive. When you speak, people will listen. So whatever you do, don't be embarrassed about your relationship with Jesus!

It doesn't matter if you stutter, speak haltingly, or slip in a southern "y'all" or a Canadian "eh." Just let your passion for Jesus come through, and that unwavering confidence will be contagious. This is not self-confidence; it's confidence in Jesus. Trust that Holy Spirit will make your words penetrate people's hearts when you share the joy you've found in Jesus.

That doesn't mean you'll reach everyone. Jesus couldn't, and neither will you. Remember that you are not responsible for the results when you share your faith. That's God's responsibility. You are responsible to be open to Holy Spirit's leading and share your story with passion and confidence.

WHO'S INTERESTED? YOU MIGHT BE SURPRISED

Sometimes when believers have a hard time influencing others to know Jesus, they develop a belief system to support the lack of interest. For example, some say, "People only come to Jesus when they hit bottom or their life is a wreck." That is sometimes the case, but I have known a great number of successful professional people who have given their lives to Christ when things were going quite well. They did face a crisis, but it wasn't one that was openly visible to the world. Their crisis was internal—they didn't know Jesus. These people gave their lives to Jesus just as readily as someone facing an illness, a divorce, or any other major life event. They simply needed someone to explain the gospel to them in a contemporary way.

We also have plenty of young people in our church, and a great variety of people from all walks of life. We can't assume people aren't interested in Jesus because of their age or the way they look. We need to be open to whomever Holy Spirit leads us to reach. After all, Jesus is for everyone!

Holy Spirit wants to introduce everyone to Jesus, but not everyone will wander into your church looking for him. We need to go looking for them, and we can't be limited by our own preconceived notions about who might be interested in Jesus, or by worrying about what our Christian friends might think.

If you're invited to a wedding or a neighborhood party where you know there's going to be a lot of drinking, you don't make yourself more holy by staying home. Of course you need to use wisdom about what situations you place yourself

> **You can't live the adventure of the Spirit Contemporary life if you are more concerned with maintaining the friends you have than with reaching out to others.**

in, but when you have an opportunity to develop relationships with people who don't yet know Jesus, don't shy away because of what your Christian friends might think. Bring a six-pack of root beer, and be the life of the party!

You can't live the adventure of the Spirit Contemporary life if you are more concerned with maintaining the friends you have than with reaching out to others. It's always worth the risk to reach out. Your job is not to hold the fort until Jesus returns. It is to look for and help guide those who are looking for God and for answers about life.

All around you there are men, women, and children who may face eternity without Christ. Will you be more open to Holy Spirit? Are you willing to be more available to others? Your efforts matter more than you know.

20 But What About the Kids?

The numbers are in, and the results are shocking. The church has done a terrible job of reaching the next generation. Some churches have missed the opportunity to reach young people by burying their head in the sand and refusing to be led by Holy Spirit in contemporary ways. Others have alienated the next generation by adding Hollywood touches to what God is doing. These attempts to "spectacularize" Holy Spirit are so detrimental. They turn off the next generation.

The emerging generation can tell when something is being exaggerated, so these tactics make them cynical toward church. They've become leery of Holy Spirit because of the strange behaviors that have been associated with him. To a great extent, an entire generation needs to be reintroduced to Holy Spirit as he really operates, and Spirit Contemporary is the answer to this problem.

Spirit Contemporary is also the answer for kids who drift away from Jesus. Many have distanced themselves from God because of the way others speak about him. They may have heard that we have to plead with God before he'll consider answering our prayers, and they can't understand why a God who loves them would make them grovel and cry to get his attention. Others are just plain tired of the judgmentalism and hypocrisy they've seen among Christians.

The Spirit Contemporary approach is an answer because it shows the next generation a truer picture of God, as modeled by Jesus. Jesus effortlessly and easily reached out with the power of Holy Spirit, and so can we. This approach gives kids a sense of the joy and beauty that comes from serving Jesus and letting Holy Spirit into their lives. The discovery of this passion for serving Jesus is especially important for second-generation Christian kids.

If you're a first-generation Christian, you likely have a clear understanding of what it means to give your life to Christ. You remember what your life was like before you met Jesus, and you know the difference he has made. You might recall the shame, condemnation, and emptiness you felt before and know the hope, excitement, and passion that came along with this new life.

Second-generation Christians have known Jesus from a young age. They've never experienced life without him. This is a tremendous advantage; however, they might take the Christian life for granted and even wander away from it.

Many times it's because these kids haven't made their relationships with Jesus personal. They've been taught right from wrong and can modify their behavior to match what's expected of them, but they haven't established a personal relationship with Christ. That's a dangerous position to be in. Some will continue to go through the motions of the spiritual life, attending church, taking part in Christian activities, and even praying, all with no sense of passion and purpose. Others will quietly disappear from the faith.

Our kids need an authentic relationship with Jesus. They need to see Holy Spirit work in their lives. When they do, their faith comes alive!

We can ensure that our kids don't fall away from Jesus by living the Spirit Contemporary life ourselves and helping them live it too. That will depend on teaching them two important concepts: (1) who God really is, and (2) who they are as followers of Christ.

Hopefully you've caught a glimpse of who God really is as you've been reading this book. He's a loving Father who cares deeply for each human being. He sent his Son, Jesus Christ, to save us, and he empowers us to live spectacular new lives through Holy Spirit within us.

The second item, who we are as followers of Christ, is the subject of this chapter. Communicating both these truths to our kids is key when it comes to reaching the next generation.

If you're a second-generation Christian and are just realizing that you've not had a firm grasp on these two points, keep reading. You can come to know Jesus in a real, passionate way, and from there you will go on to create the life of your dreams.

BREAK THE BUBBLE

Christian parents are eager, sometimes desperate, to insulate their children from the evils of the world. As a result, Christian kids often have a small circle of friends and have no idea how to interact with people beyond it. But Jesus's church was never intended to be a fortress designed to keep the world out. As Christian parents, it's our job to teach our children to thrive in that world so they can impact it! We need to stop insulating them from the world and, instead, involve them more closely in reaching out to others.

This Christian life is not just about us. Jesus's church is a rescue operation, not a cruise ship or country club. And a church youth group shouldn't be focused solely on our kids. Although it's important for our children to grow spiritually, they need to be taught to reach out to the community as well. If we don't involve our kids in reaching others for Jesus, we will rob them of lives of adventure, purpose, and fulfillment.

Having a youth group that reaches unchurched teens freaks out some Christian parents. Teenagers who are promiscuous and do drugs will end up attending the group, and that's a concern to parents who are trying to insulate their kids from the world. However, if Christian kids aren't equipped to handle relationships with those who don't share their lifestyle, even within the protective atmosphere of a church youth group, they're in trouble. They don't stand a chance of doing so at a secular university, where there are no youth leaders looking out for them.

Our kids don't need a bubble. They need to be equipped to *thrive* in the world, and they need a cause they can be passionate about. That cause is Jesus's church! When youth stay passionate about the call of God on their lives and they keep volunteering and giving of themselves to bring people to Jesus, they are much more likely to stay strong for Christ because their choices are no longer just about themselves. Not only do they make better choices but they can also make an incredible impact on their world. They rise up to achieve their God-given potential and become the devil's worst nightmare!

THE RIGHT SOURCE

Of course, a big part of equipping Christian kids to reach out to nonbelievers is giving them a solid sense of identity. The danger for Christian teens is that they can get so wrapped up in appearances that they don't know or understand what's going on inside their hearts. Christian parents unwittingly contribute to that when they focus all their attention on modifying their children's behavior. The kids naturally conclude that what they look like on the outside matters more than what they think, feel, and believe on the inside.

Parents also commonly make the mistake of labeling their kids based on their external characteristics, such as personality traits or behaviors. For example, it seems harmless to call one of the kids "our little troublemaker" if he's always pushing the limits of authority. It's also easy to label another as "the responsible one" if she always does her schoolwork. But when we label our kids, we teach them to define their identities incorrectly. Their identities run much deeper than surface tendencies or habits. Their true identities are found in Christ.

When we label our kids based on external characteristics, they assume things about themselves. The "little troublemaker" will retain that self-identification into adulthood. The girl who is told she is a perfect angel will believe she has to uphold that standard throughout her life, which is impossible. When she fails, she'll condemn herself ruthlessly.

What's even worse is when the things we say to our children give a wrong picture of who God is. For example, if a child is caught lying, we might say, "God knows when you lie," or, "Liars don't go to heaven." That's not even true! If it were, we'd all be destined for hell. Statements like this teach kids that God is vindictive, always on the lookout for a way to punish people. These fear-based motivators are destructive because they cause kids to move away from God.

A child's view of God and of himself or herself are two foundational points in life. Never sacrifice them in an effort to teach kids to behave. When they do wrong, you can use loving discipline to teach them that they are loved and that their choices have consequences. In doing so, you teach them who they really are: that their identities are defined by their relationships with Christ, not by the things they do or fail to do.

KING'S KIDS

Contrary to popular opinion, a Christian parent's job isn't to train kids to be good enough for God. When we teach our kids they need to obey God to earn his love, we're telling them that they are unacceptable as they are and that they have to change in order to earn God's love.

Nothing could be further from the truth! A Spirit Contemporary approach involves teaching them that they are unconditionally loved and valued by God. They are his kids, royalty in his kingdom, and they simply need to be who they already are. Regardless of how many times they fail, they are King's kids. They are forgiven, loved, and filled with his power. They just need to put on that new identity. They need to live out who they already are. Ephesians 4:22–24 calls this "put[ting] off your old self . . . and . . . put[ting] on the new."

We do need to teach kids proper behavior by making sure that they experience the consequences of their actions. But there's no need to wrap that discipline up with their identities or God's acceptance of them. They need to see that they are loved by their Father God, accepted through Jesus, and unconditionally forgiven. Only then will they be empowered to do right.

If you've said things in the past that negatively shaped a child's self-image, don't beat yourself up about it. We've all made our fair share of parenting mistakes. Just move forward with the resolve to help your children grow in their understanding of who God is and who they are in Christ. By doing so, you will help them grow along with you.

GIVE IT A MINUTE!

The next generation needs to see that this life of serving Jesus in a Spirit Contemporary way is an exciting adventure. It's so much better than anything the world could offer!

There's no more exciting way to live than to be guided by Holy Spirit in every moment of every day. But many youth become disinterested in following Christ because the Christians they know aren't living this way. The Christian life seems so unexciting when the only focus is to be morally good. While I'm not saying that being morally good is a bad idea, you have to admit that if that's the only thing we're living for, it makes for a pretty boring existence.

This reminds me of a beautiful teaching from John 10 that's often misunderstood. In it, Jesus compares himself to a shepherd and those who follow him to sheep. There's a wonderful truth to be found there, but some have taken the metaphor a bit too far. Sheep are not the brightest animals in the world, and though they provide a great example of what it means to follow a leader who loves and guides us, we definitely do not want to have all the characteristics of sheep.

> **Sheep are fearful and helpless for the most part, but we aren't helpless, fearful little sheep.**

Sheep are fearful and helpless for the most part, but we aren't helpless, fearful little sheep. We are children of the King! We are more than conquerors, born of God (see Romans 8:37; John 1:13). Greater is he who is in us than he who is in the world! (see 1 John 4:4). We have authority on the planet to pray and release God's power. When we speak, Holy Spirit can speak through us. Angels are camped around us, and we are empowered to bring success to whatever we put our hands to. That doesn't sound sheep-like to me! There's nothing passive or pathetic about the Spirit Contemporary life. God wants us to rise up and do his work in the world, and it's exciting!

When kids are presented with this power-packed, purpose-filled way of living, often they are the quickest to pick it up. I've heard so many stories of kids and teens at our church reaching out to the people around them and getting miraculous results. For example, one teenager who had been a believer for only about a month told me the story of how he prayed for his shop teacher during class.

The shop teacher had been showing the kids how to work on a motor that was propped up on a table. Somehow the motor slipped off its props when he was working on it, and its entire weight—somewhere between two hundred and four hundred pounds—fell directly on the teacher's hand, pinning it against the table.

The students were able to lift the motor off the teacher's hand, but it was clear that he was in a lot of pain by the way he cradled his injured hand. At that point my teenage friend piped up, and even though he was brand-new to Christianity, he prayed a quick prayer for healing in front of the entire class.

Continuing to support his hand, and with a sarcastic look on his face, the teacher said, "It still hurts."

The kid shot back, "Well, give it a minute!"

Then seconds later, the teacher's facial expression changed to shock. "The pain is gone!" he announced. Full movement and use were also restored, with the entire class looking on. This teenager was able to bring several of the guys from his class to youth group after that incident, and he didn't need to be a Bible scholar or pastor for Holy Spirit to work through him!

To reach the next generation, we need to demonstrate the life of adventure and purpose God has for each of us. Young people are looking for adventure. If they don't find it in the church, they'll find it elsewhere. It may be empty and meaningless adventure, but to them it's better than none at all. Meanwhile, a life of serving Jesus is packed with the very purpose, passion, and adventure they are seeking, and it comes from serving God all out.

NEVER GIVE UP

Being Spirit Contemporary is the key to reaching the next generation. That includes being sensitive to the questions and needs of young people. It means being aware of their hurts, challenges, and temptations. It involves speaking their language, understanding their music, and adapting ourselves to help them learn and to motivate them. More than all that, it requires making sure they have an accurate view of our awesome, loving God as well as a strong sense of their identities as his kids. It means teaching them to rely on Holy Spirit in their everyday lives in a way that's contemporary.

They do struggle with temptation; it's true. We could spend all of our time teaching them what not to do. We can, and we should, teach them to avoid drugs, alcohol, and promiscuous sexual behavior. But it is even more powerful to teach them what *to* do.

They need to know that seeking Holy Spirit will bring them peace. They need to learn to derive their self-worth from what God says about them in the Word. They need to be filled with God's love, and that's what Holy Spirit is trying to accomplish in them: show them they are loved by God and that he has beautiful lives for them. The Spirit Contemporary life is infused with incredible power, peace, and joy. Let's teach our kids to rise above shame, fear, and condemnation and live in the love and grace of God!

Kids need to know that we believe in them and that they can do great things. They need to see us living this Spirit Contemporary life. They need to be told that they can live this life too and that God has awesome things in store for them. Help them to begin this adventure of serving God every day by relying on Holy Spirit. Never give up on them! Through Holy Spirit's power, they will accomplish incredible things!

21 | Multiple Worlds

Like many of us, I can get wrapped up in my own world—the problems I'm facing and the goals I'm trying to achieve. But I need to remind myself that all the members of my family have their own worlds too—their own struggles, dreams, and daily realities. Actually, I've found that the key to being Spirit Contemporary in my own home is to connect with each of them in that world. Though I haven't always done this perfectly, I aim to be led by Holy Spirit within my own family. I try to step out of "my world" and into each of their worlds as much as I can.

At first this wasn't easy. When I worked in emergency rescue, my world included attending to suicide calls, accidents with multiple casualties, and victims of brutal violence. Because these problems seemed so big, I struggled to identify with Sally when she shared the frustrations of her world as a stay-at-home mom. While I was dealing with death and traumatic injuries, she was trying to teach the kids to pick up after themselves. I knew what she was dealing with was important, and I am in no way minimizing it. It just was hard to make the switch sometimes from the world I dealt with at work to that home world.

The same was true with each of my kids. When they were little, their school-yard problems seemed small compared with the crises I dealt with at work. But their problems were huge in their world, and rightly so. If I had been in their shoes, I would have felt no different. So I had to find a way to live in their world so I could see their problems, wins, goals, and dreams from their perspective.

One of the keys to that was learning to be truly present when we were together. All parents have problems and issues vying for their attention. I was no different. In the midst of all that, I had to switch my focus. Rather than smiling and nodding, pretending to be listening while juggling a thousand priorities in my mind, I had to focus fully on the moment and the person I was with. Thankfully, I'm getting much better at that. I love being in the moment with my family. It's one of the greatest joys of my life!

When you make the decision to enter fully into each of your loved ones' worlds, you'll start to love it. I've been able to see life through the eyes of a child and to connect with my wife on a level I never dreamed possible. I share their wins and help them walk through the losses. When I stayed wrapped up in my world, I had a tendency to lecture my kids and minimize their problems. Now I have the joy of walking through life with them, and I've been able to remain close to each of them even through their teenage years.

We all tend to become self-focused if we're not careful, which just makes us miserable. We are much more fulfilled when we look beyond our own needs and wants. The reality is that living the Spirit Contemporary life in your home means living in multiple worlds, and we all need to make a conscious effort to enter the worlds of the people we are with.

INSIDE EDGE

Holy Spirit gives you an inside edge in relating to your family, especially in raising children. For example, he'll show you when one of your kids is struggling. Kids go through seasons when wisdom seems to be lacking, and parents can't always keep a finger on everything their kids do. That's when we need Holy Spirit to guide us. He also helps us to pray for protection and leads us to ask just the right questions at the right time.

My mom was a great example of a parent led by Holy Spirit. I come from a family of five boys, and when we were teens, Mom always seemed to know when one of us was doing something we shouldn't have been. One of my brothers hid a bag of marijuana above one of the tiles in our basement ceiling. During dinner, Mom announced that she knew there was something in our house that didn't belong, and she was going to find it. We looked on dumbfounded as she went to the exact tile in the basement ceiling, moved a chair under it, and reached up to grab the hidden stash. She proceeded to march straight to the bathroom with my brother calling behind her, "Mom, don't! Wait!" Turns out he was selling the stuff and owed his dealer quite a bit of money. Before he could do anything about it, Mom had flushed the entire bag.

On another occasion she was led straight to one of my brothers' dresser drawers, where she found a hidden pornographic magazine. When she confronted him, he accused her of snooping through his belongings. She assured him that wasn't the case. She had been led directly to that drawer and even to the specific pile of clothes concealing the magazine. Given her track record, we believed her.

I know of other parents who have woken in the middle of the night with an urgent sense to pray for one of their children. Later they discovered that their child had been protected from a near accident at the exact moment they had prayed. Isn't it awesome that Holy Spirit will guide and help us to protect our families?

Holy Spirit also helps us to sense when our kids need something from us. When one of my daughters went through a period of acting out with loud, disruptive behavior, I asked Holy Spirit to show me anything I should know about. It's hard to explain, but one day when I was at work, I suddenly just knew what my daughter needed from me. I had been very serious around the family because of some of the things I had been dealing with at work, and I sensed that she needed to see me laugh. She was teasing and harassing me because she needed to break the seriousness somehow.

That night when I returned home, she met me with the same sort of behavior. Rather than reprimanding her, I tackled her to the ground and tickled her until we were both laughing. Going forward, I made a point to laugh more at home, and her behavior changed. The disruptive behavior stopped completely because of a simple little bit of advice from Holy Spirit.

When praying for your children, one of them may stand out in your mind more than usual. When this happens, find some time to talk with that child. There's a reason why Holy Spirit singles out certain people in our lives. Take that child for a walk or on an errand, and steer him or her toward opening up. You might even say

> **Holy Spirit will guide you in parenting your children.**

something like, "I've been thinking about you a lot over the past few days. What's going on?"

Holy Spirit will guide you in parenting your children. Be contemporary with your kids also, meaning, work to understand their perspective. And when it comes to your beliefs, remember that your children won't necessarily pick up your beliefs just by being around you. You need to be intentional in finding ways to communicate your faith in ways that are meaningful to them.

SHELF LIFE?

Many excellent churches have a one-generation shelf life because they fail to bring their children with them. How sad that all the wisdom gained in building a congregation is lost because it isn't passed down.

Do your values and beliefs have a shelf life? Are you investing in your church and community in ways that will benefit those who come after you? Remember, our kids won't automatically follow Jesus just because we do. In fact, it's possible for one generation to lose the entire generation that follows.

Joshua was a great leader, but he failed miserably in this area. Judges 2:10 says that after Joshua's generation passed away, "there arose another generation after them who did not know (recognize, understand) the Lord, or even the work which He had done for Israel" (AMPC). And verse 12 says, "And they forsook the Lord, the God of their fathers, Who brought them out of the land of Egypt. They went after other gods of the peoples round about them and bowed down to them, and provoked the Lord to anger" (AMPC). Despite the incredible things Joshua had done for God, he failed in this critical area. He did not bring the next generation with him, and they deserted God to serve other gods.

How could the generation that followed the mightiest of God's warriors get so far off track? We don't know all the details, but it's easy to imagine that Joshua and his leaders congratulated themselves on their great victories for God, while their children were off doing their own thing. I wonder if Joshua's generation assumed that the next generation would simply follow suit and so made no effort to pass on their sense of adventure and passion to their kids.

If so, many Christian parents are making the same mistake today.

We have to enter our kids' world and communicate our faith to them in ways they can understand. We need to share in living color and with emotion what Jesus did for us. We need to share stories with the next generation about what God did in our generation. As it says in Psalm 145:4: "Let each generation tell its children of your mighty acts; let them proclaim your power" (NLT).

The next generation walks on the shoulders of the previous one, so we also need to spur them on and expect them to be bigger and better than we are. Unfortunately, many believers actually *expect* their kids to fall away from Jesus in their teenage years! If that's what we expect, that's what we will get. Guided by Holy Spirit, we need to find contemporary ways to pass on to our children our faith, our passion, our sense of adventure, and our vision. This is our first job as parents.

EXPECT MORE!

Your beliefs as parents and leaders are critical in launching children into their destiny. Psalm 127:4 says that children are "like arrows in the hands of a warrior." Metaphorically speaking, we place our children in a bow and launch them into the world. It's our job to aim them in the right direction.

To raise up the next generation for greatness, we need to expect them to be better, do more, and reach higher than we ever have. In too many churches today, we see only gray hair. Churches that reach only one generation often take themselves off the hook by saying, "It's very difficult in this day and age," or, "It's this generation. They are just selfish." They have very low expectations of themselves and their youth. But if we want our kids to serve Jesus with passion, we have to have *higher* expectations, not lower! And we need to be purposeful.

If we are not Spirit Contemporary in dealing with our kids, relating to them where they are, they will not serve Christ. But when we make the effort to get into their world, communicating with passion and expecting much of them while equipping them to live up to those expectations, they will rise to a higher level than we could ever imagine.

22 What Faith Can't Do

When I think of the Spirit Contemporary life, two key words come to mind: *faith* and *wisdom.* To be Spirit led, we have to have faith. We need to understand how Holy Spirit leads us, and we need to be able to act on the authority we have as representatives of Jesus. And to be contemporary, we have to have wisdom. We need to grow in our ability to understand people so we can best connect with those we want to reach.

Faith and wisdom: one doesn't function well without the other. Yet many believers make the mistake of favoring either faith over wisdom or wisdom over faith. Some forget about the power Holy Spirit provides us and rely entirely on their own abilities. Others forget about wisdom and think they need a miracle to solve every problem. Both are wrong. Faith can't do what only wisdom can do, and wisdom can't do what only faith can do.

To be Spirit Contemporary, you need both faith and wisdom.

If a doctor were to give you a diagnosis, you would use wisdom to take advantage of every possible remedy available to you. At the same time, you would use faith to believe for healing. You would also trust Holy Spirit to lead you to the people and solutions you need. As a result, you might alter your diet or start exercising—acting in wisdom. One does not negate the other; wisdom and faith operate side by side. By taking action to get yourself healthy, you're not saying that you don't believe in miracles. By asking for a miracle, you're not refusing medical treatment. You trust wisdom to do its part, and faith takes care of the rest.

Belief in miracles is not an excuse to be lazy. You can't just pray for a better marriage and then refuse to go to a conference, read a book, or consult a counselor. You also can't just pray for more money and do nothing to improve your income or ability to manage your finances. Even if God dropped thousands in your lap, without wisdom you would lose it, just as many lottery winners lose their winnings because they haven't learned how to manage their money over time.

> **We are both natural and supernatural beings.**

We are both natural and supernatural beings. When you need a supernatural answer to a problem, it's there through the power of God. But if you just need natural wisdom, you need to get up and pursue it yourself, and of course, Holy Spirit will help to guide you to find it.

To grow in wisdom, you first need to build your knowledge of the topic. Proverbs (which is our go-to book in the Bible for wisdom for life) always talks about knowledge, understanding, and wisdom. Knowledge is the raw material for making a wise decision. First, you need to get the facts. But facts alone don't help you if you don't know what to do with them.

You need to gain understanding by meditating on the information. You think about those facts and decide how to apply them to your situation. Then, once you have an idea of how to apply that information, you gain wisdom when you apply your newfound understanding in the real world. All three steps are crucial. (1) Gain information. (2) Think about how to apply it. (3) Actually make changes based on what you've learned.

I'm not saying that God is not involved when you build wisdom, but you certainly have your part to play. It takes action, choices, and decisions, and it takes belief, trust in God's guidance, and faith. By balancing faith and wisdom, you will manage your life well in every area. This is critical for being Spirit Contemporary. To grow in favor with others, you need to gain their respect. That won't happen if you never grow in knowledge or skill and instead wait for God to drop everything in your lap.

Of course, none of us is perfect in this area, and you don't have to be to reach people for Jesus. In fact, putting on a mask of perfection only drives people away. But when you apply God's principles to your life with wisdom, others will notice your successful life and want to know how you do it. This gives you the perfect opportunity to point them to Jesus. Faith and wisdom working together: that's the Spirit Contemporary life.

BETTER THAN MIRACLES

The more successful you become, the more influence you will have. That makes it important to continually grow in your ability to manage your life with wisdom. Whatever you don't manage well, you lose. If you don't manage well in an area of life, you will fall back down to the last level you could manage well. For example, if you set out to lose weight but can't manage your diet and exercise routine, you'll quickly return to the weight you were when you started. If you can't manage the time and effort it takes to make your marriage strong, you'll likely go back to being single. Life management is simply *wisdom in action*.

Zig Ziglar, in his book *Over the Top: Moving from Survival to Stability, from Stability to Success, from Success to Significance,* identifies four stages of growth in any given area of life: survival, stability, success, and significance.

For example, when you begin dating someone, you're probably in survival mode. You don't yet know if the relationship is going to last. If you end up getting married, you hit stability. You promised to be together forever. However, this is not success, not yet anyway. Plenty of marriages are stable but unhappy, and plenty more don't last. To reach success you need to understand each other and have worked out your differences so that you experience true intimacy, shared goals, and a good partnership. However, this still isn't the ultimate goal of marriage.

Significance is even more important than success. That's the point when your marriage means more than just the happiness you bring each other. In a relationship of significance, you use your marriage to encourage others. You might use your experiences to help friends who are going through a tough time in their marriage, or you and your spouse might serve as a model to your kids, who will take what they learn from you into their future marriages.

Significance is the goal for every area of life, but it can come more easily in one area than another. For example, you may feel like you've hit significance in your marriage, but you're still stuck in survival mode in your finances. Or you may be in the success stage in your business but just breaking through to stability in your health. Don't let that bother you. We all have things to work on in life. Just keep learning and growing, using both faith and wisdom.

Miracles are not God's best for your life.

Many people aim for the wrong goal, assuming that the more spectacular miracles they receive, the more successful they are. That's exactly backward. Think about it for a moment. When do you need a miracle? When your business is doing well? When your marriage is happy and strong? When you're healthy and full of energy? No, you need a miracle when you're struggling. Survival miracles happen only in the survival stage, not in the stability, success, or significance stages. I'm talking about miraculous healings or provision of finances—these occur when you're really down and out, and they *are* spectacular. However, they're not God's best for your life.

Miracles stem from Holy Spirit's power, so it's easy to assume they are the goal in every situation. But it is far better to have great health than to have poor health and be kept alive by a miracle. Miracles are great when we need them, but God doesn't want us to live in survival mode. He wants us to use wisdom to manage our way to success and then significance so we can help others. We can't have influence with others if we're constantly in survival mode. We need to grow to significance by applying wisdom to our lives.

NO MAGIC WANDS

Israel's passage out of slavery in Egypt to freedom in Canaan portrays the journey from survival to significance very well. In the wilderness, the Israelites were in survival mode, and God provided for every need through incredible miracles. He created a pillar of fire to keep them warm in the cold desert night, and during the day he sheltered them from the hot sun with a cloud. Their clothes did not wear out for the forty years they lived in the desert, and God provided heavenly food called manna every morning. When they were thirsty, God instructed Moses to strike a rock, and a stream exploded from it, big enough to provide water for over two million people.

Although these miracles were wonderful, you couldn't call this stage of their journey "successful." Imagine wearing the same clothes for forty years, eating the same food three times every day, and drinking only water. These miracles kept them alive, but nothing more. They longed for their Promised Land, which was said to flow with milk and honey. But honey doesn't drop from the sky like manna, and milk doesn't pour from a rock when you hit it. Milk and honey take more than a miracle—they take work. Canaan was also flowing with giants—people the Israelites would have to fight if they wanted to possess the land!

The Israelites certainly needed faith to drum up the courage to fight those giants and live in the Promised Land, but they needed wisdom too. In Canaan they had to move from survival mode to stability, from stability to success, and from success to significance. First, they needed faith that God would take them through the wilderness and into Canaan, and the generation that initially left Egypt didn't have it. An entire generation died in that wilderness because they lacked the faith to take hold of God's promise.

When the next generation finally did fight for Canaan and took the land, the manna stopped coming and their clothes started wearing out. No longer did they hit rocks for water; they dug wells. The daily miracles they had relied on in survival mode were no longer necessary because they had access to something better, if they were willing to work for it.

I've noticed over the years that God loves to do miracles for his people. When you are in survival mode, he will stabilize your life. But if you really want to succeed, don't expect to wave a magic wand and "poof" it into existence! Success and significance come through following God's principles. To be Spirit Contemporary, you need to recognize both the spiritual and the practical sides of success. Holy Spirit will guide you and assist you, and his favor will be upon you, but you need to be ready for the increase he wants to give you. Do you have the skills to maintain it?

Sometimes we are so spiritually minded that we don't think things through. To be Spirit Contemporary, become excellent at all you put your hand to. Learn, grow, and develop skill with people at the same time you believe God will support you. Use faith and wisdom.

EXCELLENCE IS ATTRACTIVE

As you use faith and wisdom to manage every area of life well, you will move to success and then significance. You will rise in your career because of your commitment to being a lifelong learner, and you'll gain influence with others because you will gain skill at what you do. Excellence is a crucial part of being Spirit Contemporary because people are attracted to excellence.

Think about it. Would you enjoy going to a restaurant that served you stale bread and rancid butter, lukewarm soup, hard-as-a-rock steak, and cold mashed potatoes? Is that the type of place you would rave about to your friends? Or how would you like to go to a movie theatre that had broken seats, a crackly sound system, and a projector that kept cutting out? No, we all love excellence. We're attracted to it. And there's nothing wrong with that.

Excellence originates with God. He doesn't do anything in a mediocre way, and he never "just gets by." God does everything with excellence. It is his nature. Psalm 76:4 says he is "glorious and excellent" (NKJV). And this is what God says about you: you are "the excellent, the noble, *and* the glorious, in whom is all my delight" (Psalm 16:3, AMPC). God has given us the desire to grow, excel, and become more like him—more excellent!

> **People are not attracted to the words you speak until they're attracted to the life you live.**

The trouble is that many Christians seem to have a problem with excellence because they have entangled it with acceptance. Talking about excellence is a sore point for them because they feel like they can never measure up. But pursuing excellence isn't about trying to earn acceptance from God or from others. It just means that we want to be more like our heavenly Dad.

Excellence is also not the same as perfection. Perfectionists are never happy because nothing is ever perfect. But when you're committed to excellence, you do the best you can with what you have, knowing you'll always aim to improve.

When people think of Christians or of church, words like *excellent* don't come to mind, but I believe we can change this. The difference between *average* and *excellent* usually means only a few extra moments of your time and effort. It is thinking things through or proofing something one last time before presenting. It is offering to do a menial but important task that no one else wants to do.

Excellence is not difficult—it just takes commitment. And it is so worth it. It's powerfully attractive, and since Christianity is meant to be the most powerful, attractive force on the planet, it's on us to be excellent. Let's be the first place people turn to when they're looking for excellence!

———

Apply wisdom in every area of your life and work at being excellent in all you do, and you will discover the gifts God placed in you. Then develop those gifts. Grow in intelligence, in people skills, and in your ability to handle adversity. Faith will enable you to weather the storms of life, believing God will see you through. And if you are forced to take a step backward on your journey, you will only grow as a result.

So become Spirit Contemporary by applying both faith and wisdom to becoming excellent in every way you can, because people are not attracted to the words you speak until they're attracted to the life you live.

23 Live Your Two Callings

A few years ago I read a book written for successful people who had reached midlife and were searching for significance. It appealed to people who were deciding what they wanted to do with the rest of their lives and wondering if what they had done up to that point counted for anything.

This midlife phenomenon is real. It happens when people reach what they believed would be the pinnacle of success in their lives, and they realize they have been living with no purpose other than to serve themselves. Their lives suddenly seem meaningless. Many people who enter this life stage do crazy things. Some have affairs and abandon their marriages. Others quit their jobs and set out on a quest to find themselves.

Interestingly, younger generations are coming to this crisis of meaning at a much earlier age. Even many teens are disillusioned with the life of self-indulgence. They're not looking for just a career—they want a cause. They want to know that what they do with their time and energy makes some difference in the world.

The question of purpose is a timely one for a large portion of our population. Many are asking, *What is my purpose?* What's your answer? Do you know your purpose? Even born-again, Spirit-filled people can lose sight of their purpose and begin to feel empty. Make no mistake, God has a purpose for your life, and you are desperately needed to reach those around you for Christ.

The world is waiting for you to find your calling, fulfill your purpose, and live this amazing adventure called the Spirit Contemporary life.

WE ALL LONG FOR PURPOSE

Everyone feels a longing for purpose because God planted it in our hearts. Ecclesiastes 3:11 puts it this way: God has "set eternity in the human heart." Inside every person on this planet there is a longing for eternity that only God can fulfill. Money and success won't fill this craving; neither will family or relationships. There is nothing wrong with either financial and career success or great relationships, but these are not our first purpose. When we make them our number-one goal, they begin to own us. In time, we feel regret if we neglect the purposes God has for us.

There is a divine purpose planted within us that nothing else under the sun can satisfy. Only God can fill this desire. Interestingly, this deep sense of purpose isn't satisfied even by giving your life to Jesus. There are many unhappy, purposeless believers. As important as it is to know Christ, simply knowing him doesn't fulfill our longing for significance. Each of us is designed for a purpose.

Christians often mistakenly believe that only pastors and missionaries have a God-given purpose in life. Nothing could be further from the truth! Ephesians 1:11 says, "In Him we also were made [God's] heritage (portion) *and* we obtained an inheritance; for we had been foreordained (chosen and appointed beforehand) in accordance with His purpose, Who works out everything in agreement with the counsel *and* design of His [own] will" (AMPC). In other words, God has a purpose for you, and he's known about it since the beginning of time. I'm a pastor, but I'm no more called than you are. And your calling isn't necessarily in your job title.

YOU HAVE TWO CALLINGS

We are all called by God for a purpose. In fact, you have two calls on your life. One call is to your specific purpose and gifting.

Some people are called to practice medicine; others have a leading toward business or are gifted in music. This calling also pertains to your specific role in your local church. You may be a doctor or lawyer but love to help out in kids' church, for example.

Holy Spirit guides you to this specific calling, which has to do with what you do for Christ in his church and in the world. This calling is highly individual. You are called to *your* work. There are many people in the church, but not all of them are called to the same work. You have a specific calling.

The second call on your life is general. It is the same call for every believer. We are all called to share Christ with the world. Many people focus only on their specific calling, not realizing we all share the general calling to bring others to Christ. That's where the crisis of meaning comes in. You can completely fulfill your specific calling and still feel empty because you haven't been involved in the mission of bringing others to Christ.

You could be a brilliant doctor who saves many lives or an incredible musician who writes songs the whole world sings. You could even work full time for a church or other ministry, pouring your energy into worship planning or fund-raising or managing volunteers. Yet that specific call will actually destroy you if you lack the balance and foundation of pursuing the general call of bringing people to Christ. This general call will change your life if you simply pay attention to it.

You Were Designed to Catch People

Ephesians 2:10 points out that you "are God's handiwork," and there is an exciting purpose for your life, one you share with all believers. If you're open to it, pursuing this purpose will lead you to the most adventurous, fulfilling life imaginable. Let's examine this purpose step by step.

First, Jesus explained this purpose to Simon (later known as Peter) and Andrew in Matthew 4:19. Simon Peter was in his fishing boat when Jesus called him, saying, "Come, follow me . . . and I will send you out to fish for people." Jesus didn't say, "Follow me, and I'll make you a religious, boring, judgmental person." He called Simon Peter and Andrew to catch others and bring them into the kingdom, and he calls each and every disciple, including you, to do the same. You were designed to catch people.

Attracting people to Jesus is always an exciting and inviting thing. We were never meant to slap the sin out of people. Our job is to attract them to Jesus. I walked through a park recently where several guys were blasting Bible verses on speakers, and every verse they read was about hell. One held a placard that read, "He's coming back. Are you ready? If not, you're going to hell."

Not surprisingly, no one in the crowd talked to these guys. Although they were in a high traffic area with lots of passersby, nobody stopped to listen. Even as a pastor, I walked far around them because I didn't want to be associated with what they were doing. It's sad, because that's not how Jesus behaved. I challenge you to find a place in the Bible where Jesus used guilt and shame to reach someone. The only people he had harsh words for were religious people who judged others.

Jesus is calling us to catch people. When fishing, you don't use a baseball bat to hit the fish over the head. Typically, people put something on their lines to attract the fish. In the same way, we don't hit people over the head with condemning Bible verses and expect them to love Jesus. Jesus showed us a better way.

Jesus attracted people by inspiring them to pursue God as the love of their lives. The best way to fish for people isn't to make them feel bad about themselves. It is to show them the beauty and love of Jesus.

With his help, you can become an expert on loving people into his kingdom.

With his help, you can become an expert on loving people into his kingdom. And this is the essence of the Spirit Contemporary life.

Some believers hesitate to pursue our common calling to reach others for Christ because they don't think they have the personality for it. But you don't have to be an extroverted people-person to reach people for Christ. If you're an introvert, you will reach people that those loud, outgoing people never could. Your quieter, subtler approach is just what some people need. If you're open, Holy Spirit will show you how to reach the people around you in a Spirit Contemporary way—that means by working through you and your unique personality. It's really that simple. Just stay open to Holy Spirit's leading.

When you develop a lifestyle of being open to Holy Spirit, your life will be a great big adventure. Acts 10:38 says Jesus was "anointed" and went about "doing good." He healed sicknesses and performed all kinds of miracles. Everywhere you go, there is something good you can do. You can give a compliment to somebody. You can brighten the day of a waiter who is looking down. You can encourage the cashier who just had to deal with an irate customer. Jesus wants us to catch people, but that doesn't mean we should pressure them or try to control them. Just introduce them to him, and let go of the desire to control what happens next. You can't control what people decide to do with their lives, only what you will do with yours.

I was talking to a man after church one Sunday—a guy with long hair, arms full of tattoos, wearing a motorcycle jacket. He told me he talks about Jesus with the guys at work, and it reminded me that every one of us is uniquely positioned to reach a different group of people. This man, who seems outwardly so different from me, loves the same Jesus I do, and he will reach people I never could. He said the guys he comes into contact with are typically tired of religion, but they get curious when they see how his life is different from theirs. They ask if he is religious, and he says, "No, but I have a relationship with God. I'm a free man." What an intriguing response! If they show interest, he then has an opportunity to tell them how Jesus can make you free.

You see, reaching people for Jesus is simply a matter of letting them in on the phenomenal lives they could have through Jesus, and you'll find that living this way will bring incredible meaning to your life.

JESUS IS BUILDING IT—ARE YOU IN?

Jesus taught us to seek first God's kingdom and his righteousness. When we do that, everything we need will be given to us as well (see Matthew 6:33). We can't seek pleasure, money, family, or career first, then expect to find meaning in life. We need to seek God first. Whatever you seek first—that is, what you set as your primary aim in life—eventually becomes your god. It begins to make your decisions for you.

For example, if your career is first, you'll work instead of spending time with family or going to church. If there's an extra shift available that conflicts with church or a family gathering, your decision has already been made. You'll choose the thing you have already decided is most important in your life.

Some people go after pleasure first. They'll choose what's easiest or most satisfying for themselves every time. They don't realize that pleasure makes a terrible god. God designed pleasure to follow you, not for you to seek it. Pleasure will follow you in a beautiful way if you put the kingdom first.

Let's look deeper at this matter of putting the kingdom first. In Matthew 16:18, Jesus told Simon, "Now I say to you that you are Peter (which means 'rock'), and upon this rock I will build my church, and all the powers of hell will not conquer it" (NLT). This is the first recorded time Jesus used the word *church*. The Greek word used here is *ecclesia,* which means "the called-out ones." With this statement, Jesus laid the foundation stone for *his* church, which he is building right up to this day. So if we are followers of Jesus and wish to put him first in our lives, we need to love his church as well.

It has become popular in some circles to speak poorly of the church. Church bashing is a popular sport with many players, both inside and outside the church. It's tempting to believe we can be followers of Jesus Christ yet feel contempt for the church he created and inhabits. But we can't. If we love Jesus, we need to love his church also. He loves it, he gave his life for it, and it is the only thing identified in the Bible that Jesus is building. So if we claim to love Jesus, we need to devote ourselves to his first love also—the church.

You need other believers, both for your own needs and for theirs, and to help you to reach out to others. You can lead someone to Christ, but you can't be there for every moment of the person's life. You would burn yourself out trying to meet all of that person's social and spiritual needs. The beauty of a group of believers is it can help to meet those needs.

The church is meant to be a group of people working together to train and support one another so they can learn to know God better and serve him more effectively. When you reach people for Jesus while tapped into a team like that, there's no limit to the number of lives you can help change. You will live out your own purpose best in the context of a Spirit Contemporary church.

STAY OPEN

When you live an authentic, Spirit Contemporary life, you'll find that people are attracted to you just as you are. Just be who you are, but keep your eyes wide open. Have your antenna up. You never know when God will bring across your path someone you can reach for Christ.

I was sitting on a plane one day when the lady beside me struck up a conversation. She was very well dressed and well spoken, and I discovered that she was a Christian but couldn't stand going to church. Nothing that happened there seemed to have any relevance to her. As the conversation went on, I learned she held a prominent position in a large, successful company. I later learned she was in the top 2 percent of the wealthiest people in her country. She loved Jesus but couldn't find a church that seemed meaningful to her.

I have heard that often from very successful people, and I'm convinced it is because they so frequently feel judgment from the church. The church often communicates that wealth is evil and poverty is godly, so successful people feel unwelcome there. While it's true that some successful people are consumed with money, I know plenty of wealthy people who are extremely generous with what they have. They certainly don't seem to be in love with their money because they keep using it to bless others! At the same time, I've met people with very little money who certainly seem to be consumed by it because money is all they can think about! Whether or not someone is in love with money is determined by the beliefs and attitudes they have toward money, not by their net worth.

As I spoke with this woman on the plane, I steered the conversation toward a few churches I knew of near her home that I thought she might enjoy. She was delighted by the information because she hadn't even known they existed. Moments like these are God moments, and they can happen everywhere you go.

Ecclesiastes 3:11 says God planted eternity in our hearts but adds that "no one can fathom what God has done from beginning to end." In other words, our brains will never be able to fully understand all that God is doing or how important our role in it is. You can't even imagine how many lives you've touched from the beginning of your life until now. Every kind word and action, every gift to a good cause, each time you influenced someone through your example, all the people who gave their lives to Christ because they saw in you something they wanted—you won't realize all that until you reach heaven.

So follow Jesus in the Spirit Contemporary way. Be open to people. Be open to Holy Spirit's guidance. He will lead you into a life of purpose. When you live this way, something inside you changes. You feel amazing when you know Holy Spirit is working with you, leading you to opportunities to help make a change in someone else's life.

God arranged for me to sit beside that woman on the plane. He knew before the world began that I would talk to that one woman for one hour and help her find a church, and he arranges these opportunities for you too. He may set you up in a certain line in the grocery store so you can talk to one young girl who is having a particularly frustrating day. When you encourage her, she may be floored to think that you cared enough to go out of your way to brighten her day. *Could it be that God is looking out for me?* she might think.

It's really that simple. Just keep your eyes wide open to the people around you, and step into the exciting purpose God has for your life!

Live Big

The gospel is powerful because it shows us how to be right with God. Jesus makes us right with God, and that sets us free! This isn't something you can earn. That's why Jesus came down so hard on the judgmental attitude of the religious people he encountered. They expected people to earn their way to being right with God through perfect behavior. That's impossible. Salvation is all grace.

So when believers look down their noses at others and make judgments about who is more righteous, it shows they really don't understand the gospel. Righteousness is a gift from God, and when you believe that, you become truly free. When you present Jesus this way to others, they will flock to the freedom. It's thrilling to be involved in helping others find freedom in Christ.

It is a great mistake to base our lives only on receiving great things from God.

That leads to an empty, hollow existence. Focusing on yourself is a pathway to heartache. There is a greater purpose behind your blessings—it's to bring others with you into this blessed life you're living.

God has planted within you a longing for eternal purpose that only he can fill. Jesus guides us to that purpose. Look at his example, and listen to Holy Spirit's leading. Then you'll learn how to touch people's hearts and imaginations for God. You will build something far greater than a career—you'll build a Spirit Contemporary church.

The church can meet in a building, on a street corner, under a tree, in someone's house, or in a bar during off hours. It doesn't matter where believers gather. When we come together to build this thing called church, we can do great things together. Your purpose is tied to the church. The purpose behind your business is tied to building Jesus's kingdom. So is the purpose behind your marriage and your family. If your business or your family or even your marriage is only about you and the people closest to you, you will feel a perpetual sense of emptiness and you will raise princes and princesses who think the world revolves around them. But if you will seek first the kingdom of God and his righteousness and teach your family to do the same, the good things you desire will come your way—in the right way.

Today I am asking you to make a decision. Determine you will not be a self-focused Christian who cares only about what the church can do for you and your family. Choose not to look for your sense of purpose in your marriage, family, or career. Instead, determine to follow Jesus and seek him first. Accept his purpose for your life. Decide you will find your greatest fulfillment in bringing others to Jesus. When you do, the other good things you desire will be given to you as well.

Paul's prayer was this: "I want to know Christ—yes, to know the power of his resurrection and participation in his sufferings, becoming like him in his death, and so, somehow, attaining to the resurrection from the dead" (Philippians 3:10–11). Paul wanted something far greater for himself than simply to live a comfortable, stress-free life. He hungered to enter the life of Christ, to join him in his mission, even in his suffering, and thereby to find a much higher calling. This is the Spirit Contemporary life.

As I think of the life of Paul, I realize that one person filled by Holy Spirit can change the course of an entire nation. I wonder what God could accomplish through five Spirit Contemporary people. What about a hundred, or a thousand? What if an entire church or denomination were willing to be led by Holy Spirit in contemporary ways? We can't imagine the impact it would have on this continent, on this planet, for generations to come.

This is your time. Love your life, and live it big.

That all begins with you. It is your turn to rise up and say, "No more!" to the epidemic of church closures in our nations. It is your turn to say, "I'll go!" to reach out to a generation of young people who are disaffected, dispassionate, and de-churched.

This is your time. Love your life, and live it big. As you do, bring everyone you can with you. Be filled with Jesus's compassion, and be continually open to helping others find their way with God. Seek Holy Spirit's guidance, and act on it using the gifts and personality that God has given you.

The world is waiting for you to rise up and live the Spirit Contemporary life!

Appendix

Spirit Contemporary Church

We'll never reach the world for Christ without life-giving churches. To be successful in the mission Jesus gave us, we need Spirit Contemporary churches filled with Spirit Contemporary leaders who model, teach, and train believers how to reach this hurting world.

The problem is that the church is ineffective when it exists as an isolated subculture that has little to no interaction with the world. Jesus did not design church that way. The church was never intended to be so strange and foreign that newcomers felt awkward being there. It was never meant to be a place of judgment. And it was not designed to be so out of touch with real life that it only offers answers to questions that no one is asking. The church should be a place that clearly demonstrates what Jesus is really like. Jesus loved people just as they were, his teachings dealt with real-life issues, and he knew how to connect with people from all walks of life, so that's what churches need to do too.

As we've already discussed, at Springs Church we use the acronym LAF to identify the culture we value. It's a culture of *loving, accepting,* and *forgiving.* I love the fact that this acronym is pronounced "laugh" because it creates an atmosphere of joy. This is crucial because it seems that joy and laughter have been banned from many churches.

The truth is that church should be filled with laughter! People should feel better just walking through the doors of the church because of all the smiling faces greeting them. People love to go to happy places like Disney World. They stream to movie theatres, beautiful shopping malls, and attractive coffee shops. Why can't church be one of the happy places that people can't resist going to?

It can be! And when churches represent Jesus well, people feel loved, accepted, and forgiven when they walk in, even though their lives are not perfect. Church becomes a place of joy that people can't wait to visit every Sunday.

Any other atmosphere is counterproductive for leading people to Christ. Unless people feel loved, accepted, and forgiven, they won't pay attention long enough to allow their hearts to change. People's hearts open only when they feel accepted just as they are. Only then can they accept Jesus as their Savior and Lord and truly change, because Jesus is the one who changes them—from the inside out. Shame and condemnation don't change anyone. They only drive people deeper into sin and further away from God. So we need to create churches that love people the way they are, accept them where they are, and forgive them when they fail.

Your church can become a powerfully attractive place for newcomers. That's a Spirit Contemporary church, and in that environment, people will thrive and the church will grow.

TEACH IT

Creating a Spirit Contemporary church begins with teaching people how to work with Holy Spirit in a contemporary way. There are many churches working with Holy Spirit in awkward and weird ways. This causes people to cringe and never bring friends or family with them. As Spirit Contemporary leaders, we need to teach people to operate in God's power in a way that is natural, relevant, and contemporary.

When we do this, people will be attracted to Holy Spirit when they see him at work in our services and in our lives. They'll see that he heals people, sets them free from sins, gives joy, and brings answers to difficult situations. They'll see that he guides them through complex problems, favors them, and reveals truth to them. The truth of what Holy Spirit is really like is powerfully attractive to everyone, believers and nonbelievers alike.

In our church services and our church culture, we need to pray for people as Holy Spirit leads and empowers us but to do so in a way that is relevant and contemporary. There's no need to add dramatic language or theatrics to our services, as if we needed to dress up Holy Spirit to make him seem more spectacular or powerful. Holy Spirit's power speaks for itself. We only succeed in alienating nonbelievers when we make our services a sideshow or carnival. Lift up Jesus. Listen to Holy Spirit. Relate to people with respect and wisdom. No dramatic touches are needed.

This Spirit Contemporary life is spreading around the world. People are working with Holy Spirit in a new way, without lifting themselves up or making themselves look special or important. They are making sure people see that Jesus is the one who makes the difference in their lives, not human ingenuity or power. And because Spirit Contemporary people seem so normal and natural, many others have realized that they, too, can be used by God. They can pray for people and help introduce people to Jesus. They can see miracles in their world every day because anyone can be led by Holy Spirit.

Pastors and church leaders need to equip the saints for the work of the ministry (see Ephesians 4:11–13). That means showing them how to sense and release God's power into situations. As we make working with Holy Spirit natural and easy, and when it's done in a way that attracts rather than repels people, we see the gospel message explode around the world. Everywhere Jesus's disciples went, great miracles happened, and those miracles awed people. Yet the disciples didn't glorify themselves. They gave all credit to God. When clergy are the stars of the show, the message they convey is that *they* are special somehow. And the greater the gap between the clergy and the laity, the harder it is for our churches to become Spirit Contemporary.

As leaders, we can see miracles happen in our everyday lives, we can introduce people to Jesus, and we can experience success in business and the secular world. The power of Holy Spirit in our lives isn't just to do church. We need to teach people how to use the power of the Spirit in the boardroom, on the shop floor, in the patrol car, in the classroom, and at the dinner table. The power of God is in us so that we can do our jobs better in every area of life. When God adds his super to our natural, we have the ability to do incredible things.

Create Atmosphere

Our church isn't perfect, but we continually work hard at creating a warm, friendly atmosphere that is designed specifically to put newcomers at ease. Right from the parking lot through to when they leave the building, we try to think through every part of the journey from their perspective.

When someone steps onto your church property for the first time, you have a matter of minutes to make a first impression, and that first impression has a huge influence on whether or not they ever set foot on your property again. The truth is that their first thoughts about your church are already established long before the worship team plays the first chord or the pastor speaks a word.

Have they been greeted by smiling faces several times in those first few minutes? Did a friendly parking attendant show them where to park? Did they feel lost when they got inside the building? Or did someone help them find the kids' classes, the bathrooms, and the sanctuary?

Was the décor of the building inviting? Or did it look outdated and neglected? What was the lighting like? Was any music playing in the background to set the mood? Were the bathrooms clean? Did the kids' church volunteers seem excited to meet their children? Did someone offer to help new folks find seats?

Creating an inviting atmosphere isn't difficult, but it does take some thought. You see, a Spirit Contemporary church is focused on sharing the gospel with those who have never heard it or responded to it yet. It appeals to people who have never set foot in a church before. That means a Spirit Contemporary church creates services that attract people to Jesus. They are churches where people want to be.

It's also critical that we can duplicate our behavior in church on the streets. We need to have a way of speaking, a vocabulary, and even mannerisms that work as well in a coffee shop or a business meeting as they do in the sanctuary. Everything we do in church models and equips people to share the gospel and pray for people, so everything we do in church has to work outside the church as well. If it does, people will be empowered to go out into their everyday lives and be phenomenally successful at transforming the lives of the people around them.

If we create church services that are just theatrical productions or that indulge in behavior people could never duplicate in their homes, schools, or offices, we set people up for failure. For example, I love listening to beautiful worship music and seeing people join in a sense of awe as we pray for miracles while some gather at the front of our church. But I also teach people how to pray in ordinary settings without worship music or a team of believers surrounding them in prayer. We can love the church rituals we've become accustomed to because they have deep meaning for us. Yet we need to also be able to pray with others and share our faith in everyday life.

Many people have backed away from Holy Spirit and the power he could so easily release into their lives because they've seen it demonstrated in weird ways or seen it faked or contrived. We need to be authentic. We have to allow God to work with us in a way that lets people sense his presence. We don't need to exaggerate or try hard to make God look good. He is quite capable of doing that himself.

REMOVE THE CRINGE FACTOR

Years ago at Springs Church we began to consciously remove anything that evoked what we call "the cringe factor." The cringe factor describes any of the little things that may occur in a church service that cause embarrassment or make people feel uncomfortable. If your church has a cringe factor, people think, *I'll never bring my unbelieving friend to church with me because I know* that *is going to happen.*

Over the years, I've had to confront more than a few well-meaning church members about their behavior in church. Some loved to worship by dancing wildly in the aisles; others wanted to interrupt the service to announce that they had heard something from God that they needed to share.

You might be thinking, *Leon, how could you tell people to stop this kind of thing? What if it really was God trying to speak through them?* The truth is I don't tell them that what they are doing is wrong; I just tell them to save it for later. If they feel closest to God when they're dancing wildly, great! They can do it at home where it won't distract newcomers from having their own experiences with God. And if they hear something from God that I need to know, they can catch me after the service is over to tell me. I simply redirect their attention to consider the brand-new person's perspective. Not all of them understand, and some end up leaving the church, which is too bad. But we can't cater to the few if it means we lose the opportunity to bring even one new person to Christ!

We need to be aware of the cringe factor in our personal interactions as well. We don't help God out when we make ourselves seem strange or unapproachable. Holy Spirit doesn't want our neighbors to feel judged in our presence. He is not responsible for strange behavior that makes others feel uncomfortable. There are contemporary ways to access all the power and beauty of Holy Spirit, and they don't diminish his effectiveness one bit!

One way to avoid the cringe factor is to stop speaking *Christianese*, the language only Christians understand. Throwing words like "glory," "hallelujah," and "amen" into our everyday speech is as confusing to nonchurchgoers as if we interjected words of a foreign language into our sentences as we spoke to them. It doesn't mean anything to them, and it just seems strange. And using terms like "saved," born again," "blood of the Lamb," "hedge of protection," and "walk with the Lord" may make sense to us, but not to others. If we're going to share our faith with people who are unfamiliar with Christianity, we need to translate Christian concepts into language anyone can understand, both in our everyday lives and in church.

I used to think that every church should have two kinds of services: *seeker* services, which are sensitive to new attendees, and *believer* services, during which the believers are free to pray in the Spirit, study more complicated doctrine, and prophesy. During the believer services, the cringe factor was very high. So when dealing with new believers it was difficult to transition them from the seeker service to the believer service. And if they failed to make the transition because it all seemed too strange for them, they just stopped attending altogether.

This problem really bothered me, and I wondered how to appeal to guests while also teaching the deeper things of God. Then one day it hit me: *Jesus didn't have this problem.* Jesus was able to relate to ordinary people while teaching deep spiritual truths. When I realized that, we changed things so all our services would appeal to guests. We removed all the words that nonbelievers don't understand and modeled a normal, Spirit Contemporary way of speaking and teaching. In doing so, I found I could teach about all the deeper things of God while appealing to those who were unfamiliar with the church. And not one bit of his power was lost.

Think Like a Guest

When Springs Church began growing rapidly, we were meeting in a rented facility. That meant finding a way to do two services in quick succession. One timesaver we came up with was to stop asking people to come up to the front of the church to give their lives to Christ. Instead, we had them simply raise their hands to indicate they were praying to receive Christ.

To our surprise, we saw a large increase in salvation decisions. Some people thought it was because we were compromising by not requiring people to make a public declaration of their faith. But as I talked to these new converts, especially to the men, I found that their decisions were solid. They had been waiting to make their commitments because they weren't sure what would happen when they walked down the aisle to the front.

Those of us who were longtime church members thought nothing of asking people to come forward to give their lives to Christ. It was just a way to publicly state the decision to follow Christ. However, some newcomers were concerned about what that public confession of sinfulness would communicate to others. Some were prominent business leaders and members of Parliament who had spent their adult lives building up good names for themselves. They were concerned that by walking down the aisle they were admitting to being dishonest. An accountant who had clients in attendance worried that they would think he had cheated them. These people's reputations were important to them, and there's nothing wrong with that. The Bible says that a good name is to be desired more than riches, silver, or gold (see Proverbs 22:1). As upstanding members of society, they had done their best to be good people their entire lives. They understood that they had the nature of sin and needed Jesus in order to be right with God. They just didn't want to appear in Monday's headlines.

It's easy to assume that everyone is thinking what we're thinking and understands what our rituals mean, but they don't, especially in Canada, which is a very secular country, and increasingly in the United States as well. What began as a way to save time in a very crowded morning schedule turned out to be a key to making newcomers feel more at ease, which resulted in a huge number of decisions for Christ.

It's funny because we think that we can't change the way things are being done because we'll be compromising. Meanwhile, our unwillingness to change often *is* a compromise! We sacrifice souls in heaven to hang on to what's familiar and comfortable. Enough is enough. We need to make sure we think like a guest *every* Sunday morning. I guarantee that your first-time visitors do!

———

When the church becomes a place where people are loved, accepted, and forgiven, when it's filled with joy, laughter, and relevant teaching, when the gospel is presented in a way that people understand, when the worship of God is inclusive to all, and when church traditions are understandable, then the church will thrive. In other words, a Spirit Contemporary church will be a healthy, vibrant, growing church. And it has the power to transform the world.

Study Guide

 **SESSION 1: THE PROBLEM**

Key Scripture

"I have become all things to all people so that by all possible means I might save some" (1 Corinthians 9:22).

Major Takeaways

- Church is not—it can't be—the only place God works.
- Christianity is meant to be the most powerful, attractive force on the planet.
- The answer to the problem of the declining church lies with allowing Holy Spirit to work through us in contemporary ways in the context of our normal, everyday lives.

Discussion

1. Discuss this statement: "The biggest problem the church faces today is the way we as Christians approach the rest of the world on God's behalf."
2. Have you ever witnessed Jesus being represented in a way that was confusing or off-putting to someone who didn't yet know him? Discuss how the situation might have been approached differently.
3. First Corinthians 14:1 says we can "desire spiritual gifts," but it also says to "pursue love" (NKJV). Why do you think it's important to make sure you are pursuing love when it comes to being led by God?

4. Discuss this statement: "Nowhere in the Bible does it say you have to behave strangely to be led by Holy Spirit."

5. What are some simple ways God has guided or led you to help others in your normal, everyday life?

Suggested Reading

In the next session, we'll be discussing chapters 5 to 8. I encourage you to read all the chapters, but if time is short and you may not get through them all, start with chapters 6 and 7.

 **SESSION 2: FREE TO CHANGE**

Key Scripture

"Then you will know the truth, and the truth will set you free" (John 8:32).

Major Takeaways

• Things that make you uncomfortable aren't necessarily wrong.
• Five reasons people resist change: pride, fear, rebellion, laziness, and ignorance.
• If you want to go to places you've never been, you'll have to think things you've never thought.

Discussion

1. Discuss the five reasons we resist change. Which of the five do you think may be holding you back from becoming more Spirit Contemporary?

2. Judgment and condemnation push people away from wanting to know Jesus. Have you experienced or witnessed this in your life?

3. Describe a "holy cow" you once had in your belief system and how challenging it changed your relationship with God or your approach to sharing your faith.

4. If you want to live the Spirit Contemporary life, you need to let the truth of God's Word challenge your misbeliefs. Discuss how you plan to achieve this.

5. How does having an "eternity mind-set" change your focus in life?

Suggested Reading

In the next session, we will be discussing chapters 9 to 11. To prepare for the discussion questions, be sure to read chapter 9 at minimum.

 **SESSION 3: FREE TO LIVE**

Key Scripture

"Are you tired? Worn out? Burned out on religion? Come to me. Get away with me and you'll recover your life. I'll show you how to take a real rest. Walk with me and work with me—watch how I do it. Learn the unforced rhythms of grace. I won't lay anything heavy or ill-fitting on you. Keep company with me and you'll learn to live freely and lightly" (Matthew 11:28–30, MSG).

Major Takeaways

- You already have everything you need within you to be Spirit Contemporary.
- We're taught to be meek like Jesus, but this doesn't mean we're to be timid, soft-spoken, wimpy doormats. Meekness is power under control. That's what Christians are to be like!
- Jesus came to end religion, not start another one.

Discussion

1. Discuss this statement: "I believe Jesus would be kicked out of many churches today because he would be considered un-Christlike."

2. How is Jesus "dangerous"?

3. What does it really mean to be meek?

4. How is confidence different from pride?

5. Sharing your faith is about influencing others to want to know Christ. How is this influence different from manipulation?

6. Which of the four areas (IQ—intelligence quotient; SQ—spiritual quotient; AQ—adversity quotient; EQ—emotional quotient) would you like to grow in your life? What is your plan to do this?

7. What are some ways you can grow in favor with others? And why is this important when it comes to sharing your faith?

Suggested Reading

In the next session, we will be covering chapters 12 to 14. Please read through chapters 12 and 13 at minimum to prepare for the discussion questions.

 **SESSION 4: ALL SPIRIT**

Key Scripture

"The spirit of man is the candle of the LORD, searching all the inward parts of the belly" (Proverbs 20:27, KJV).

Major Takeaways

- God can and does operate in all his power in our lives but in a way that is normal and natural for the individual. He is not limited to our preconceived notions of what his power should look like.
- Living the Spirit Contemporary life involves learning to identify and trust your internal sense of Holy Spirit's leading.
- Spirit Contemporary is a *you* thing; it's God working in *you* and through *you*. And that's incredibly powerful to the people around you.

Discussion

1. Discuss this statement: "Some have confused the work of Holy Spirit with the outward reaction to that work."

2. When we put on a show that brings attention to ourselves, how does it affect the people Holy Spirit is trying to touch?

3. There are many ulterior motives people can have for pretending that they have heard something from God. Discuss a few and share if you have ever been tempted to exaggerate.

4. Discuss how the motto "Less of me, more of Jesus" can help to shape how you interact with people when Holy Spirit is working through you.

5. You can often sense Holy Spirit's leading as a gut feeling. If you received this kind of leading at work, describe how you might share that with your coworkers in a Spirit Contemporary way.

6. Some Christians are very aware of God's leading in their everyday lives. Others are very aware of how the people around them feel. The goal is to be great at both. Share which of the two you may need to work on and how you plan to go about it.

Suggested Reading

In the next session, we will be covering chapters 15 to 18. To be prepared for the discussion questions, you'll want to read through chapters 16 and 17 at minimum.

 ## SESSION 5: ALL CONTEMPORARY

Key Scripture

"And Jesus grew in wisdom and stature, and in favor with God and man" (Luke 2:52).

Major Takeaways

- We need favor with people—rapport, relationship, trust, admiration—to impact their lives.
- The most powerful way to grow in favor with others is to respect them.

- Three key characteristics we all need to embody in our relationships with others can be summed up with the acronym LAF: love, accept, and forgive.

Discussion

1. In what ways have you seen Christians bulldoze ahead to share their faith with someone before doing the work of gaining favor with that person? What was the result?

2. Discuss the "green apples" analogy used to describe those who aren't yet ready to make a decision for Christ. How can you tell if someone is a green apple?

3. Have you felt pressured to "close the deal" when sharing your faith with others? Discuss how this urgency among Christians can be both a benefit and a detriment to sharing our faith.

4. What does LAF stand for? Discuss how having a LAF culture in your church might impact people who step through its doors for the first time.

5. How do you think Jesus grew in favor with man? Discuss how you might try this in your own life.

6. What is your testimony? If someone asked you why you follow Jesus, what would you say in two minutes or less? Take some time between now and the next session to jot down a few thoughts.

Suggested Reading

In the next session, we will be discussing chapters 19 to 23. At minimum, you will want to read through chapters 20, 22, and 23 to prepare for the discussion questions.

 **SESSION 6: RISK IT AND LIVE IT**

Key Scripture

" 'Come, follow me,' Jesus said, 'and I will send you out to fish for people' " (Matthew 4:19).

Major Takeaways

- We can ensure that our kids don't fall away from Jesus by living the Spirit Contemporary life ourselves and by teaching them two important concepts: (1) who God really is, and (2) who they are as followers of Christ.
- Our kids don't need a bubble. They need to be equipped to thrive in the world, and they need a cause they can be passionate about. That cause is Jesus's church!
- Faith can't do what only wisdom can do, and wisdom can't do what only faith can do.
- The world is waiting for you to find your calling, fulfill your purpose, and live this amazing adventure called the Spirit Contemporary life!

Discussion

1. To a great extent, an entire generation needs to be reintroduced to Holy Spirit as he really operates. How could Spirit Contemporary be the answer to this problem?
2. The key to being Spirit Contemporary in your own home is to connect with each member of your family in their world. What are some ways to achieve this?
3. Discuss the statement: "Miracles are not God's best for your life."
4. What does the following statement mean to you? "People are not attracted to the words you speak until they're attracted to the life you live."
5. Reflect on what you have learned from this book. Have any of your beliefs been challenged?
6. Has your perception of living the Christian life changed? If so, how?

Acknowledgments

Thank you to all my children, who live out this message so naturally.

Thank you to Janice Burnett. Your tireless work on this book night and day is such a gift from God.

Thank you to the Springs Church team. Together we continue to learn to be effective in this world for Christ. Sally and I love you with all our hearts.